The Deeds you Need to
Convert
Leads
to
Committed
Customers

The

Lemon Aid
Deed Alphabet

Christie Northrup
The Lemon Aid Lady

Cover design by Steve James

CANet Publishing
Dallas, Texas 75065

Juicy Profits!
Christie 2003

PUBLISHED BY CANet Publishing

Printed in the United States of America

ISBN: 1-930182-02-3

Dedicated to
my parents,
Stan and LaRae Anderson

...who taught me human relation skills—a great asset in any profession—as well as a sense for business and personal growth.

If leads are the seeds of my business, what deeds do I need to grow my seeds into a profitable business?

Do you have names and phone numbers of people who have expressed a desire to buy your product or service, or join your team? You know they are interested (or at least they were at some time) in what you offer because they invited you to contact them by giving you their name, phone number, and/or address.

Getting leads is just the beginning of growing a business—the seeds. This book, the second of the Lemon Aid Books, teaches you how to plant and nourish the seeds and convert them to long-term customers, resulting in residual profits. You literally have the seeds of a profitable business in your hands.

So, what do you do next? As with any planting, the soil and environment are critical in the successful development of a seed. As you read the following pages, you will discover ideas for creating a positive selling environment by focusing on your lead's needs—not on your reward. Just as every type of seed, and then each individual seed is unique, you'll learn that each customer is different and can't all be treated the same way.

Not all seeds will grow; just as not all leads turn in to customers. Don't fret about these. Continue to give nourishment, sunshine, and water to those who do take root, this is following through and servicing a customer.

As your seeds grow into business and residual profits, inside each piece of fruit or flower will be other seeds. These are referrals you can get from your customers to continue your relationship with them and their family and friends. There is no end to your success in teaching people what you have to offer.

Lemon Aid Terms:
NAPEF is a made-up fruit; it stands for Name, Address, Phone, E-mail, and Fax. This is the information you must have from someone who wants your product so you can contact, follow through, and service.

Throughout the book, you'll read about doing a *TWIST*. This is not a dance. It stands for **The Way I See Things**. If you experience a "sour situation" in your life and business, do the *TWIST*. This is simply the way you look at the situation. Change your view just slightly and you'll change the results. You'll *TWIST* those sour situations into Sweet Successes and Juicy Profits. And, by doing a slight *TWIST,* you'll set yourself apart from the "cookie cutters" in your industry and company so that your customers will remember You!

As your business grows, and even if you experience some "rocky" soil, e-mail me at lemonaidlady@yahoo.com or join my on-line list: onelist.com/subscribe/lemonaidlady to share your growing experiences!

Looking forward to hearing all about your Sweet Successes and Juicy Profits as you implement these ideas in your life and business.

Christie Northrup
The Lemon Aid Lady
April 1999

A

AAA: Attract, Ask, and Act

At this point in your business, you have **attracted** potential customers and have their name, phone, and/or address. This is called a Lead. The next deed in converting the leads to customers is to **ask** the lead some questions. This asking will help you assess how your product/service will help solve a situation the lead is involved in or simply enhance his/her life. Knowing more about a person will help you determine the solution the lead is looking for.

After you know you have the solution to the lead's situation, **act** on this information and invite the lead to do business with you! I am so amazed at salespeople who tell me about a new prospect, yet they have only **attracted** business and haven't begun the **asking** and **acting** stages.

If you are really nervous about asking questions and acting on the lead's responses, combine the asking and acting and simply ask the lead to take action by purchasing your product/service. This is not as effective as asking probing questions to expand your sales options, but if you ask enough people, you will get results.

One of my favorite "asking" stories is about a man selling pens at the corner of a busy downtown intersection. First of all, you might wonder why someone would sell pens on a street corner when customers can go to any convenience or office supply store and buy them.

If you aren't convinced that a person could make money selling pens in this manner, read the next section on Abundance Attitudes before reading the story.

> As people are bustling and hurrying on their way to work, the man stands at his corner and individually asks as many people as he can, "Do you want to buy a pen?" Most tell him "no;" however, many agree and make the purchase.
>
> A vice-president of the Acme Pen Company observes this man's persistence day after day and admires his tenacity. The executive knows he can help this man become more effective, so he invites the pen salesman to lunch. During lunch, the vice president compliments the pen man on his determination. And then he offers the pen man a position with the Acme Pen Company. In extending the offer, the executive tells the pen man that he will go through an extensive and expensive training course. He is promised benefits like insurance, stock options, and paid vacations. And, then the clincher, the VP offers the pen man a nice, big salary of $98,000 a year!! Taking a pen out of his suit pocket, primed to have the pen man sign the offer, the vice president hears, "But I'm already making $120,000 a year doing what I'm doing now. Do you want to buy a pen?"

We can learn many lessons from this story. But, on the subject of asking, you can learn that the easiest way to convert a lead to a customer: Simply Ask!! And it is simple. All you have to do is open your mouth.

After you are accustomed to *asking for the order,* you will be more comfortable *asking questions about the person* and his/her wants/needs/desire. Then you can achieve larger sales at greater frequencies because you will ask the right questions.

A great example of this is a salesman who helped me and my husband purchase a modular bookcase. We had just moved to a new home and were in desperate need of bookshelves. We were looking for a moderately-priced, well-made set. Every time we drove by a furniture store, we stopped in to see if we could find a match. This exercise was getting tiresome, and we needed a place for the many, many books we have collected.

One day my husband saw an advertisement for well-made, unfinished furniture. He drove to the store and found exactly what he was looking for. He was anxious to take me with him to approve his discovery.

When we returned, the salesman, Bart, recognized my husband, Bob, right away. This recognition amazed me because the first and only time Bob met Bart was on his way home form work, and he was dressed in a business suit. This was a weekend, and Bob was in his yard grubbies. But, Bart remembered him! I was impressed!

Upon examining my husband's great find, we learned the store was out of stock on one of the pieces of the modular set *we thought* we needed. We were trying to solve the problem between the two of us. Bart politely interrupted our conversation by **asking a key question:** How long is the wall where the bookcases will be ? We hadn't thought of that simple question. Instead, we were looking at the color, shape, and design of the bookshelves; not considering the *fit* along the wall. We were trying to get the shelves to match our wants—not the wall. Bart, through a simple question, reminded us of a critical need. After all, the wall was already in the house. The length of the wall could not be changed, but the length of the bookshelves could be adapted using the right modular pieces.

The question Bart asked was so simple. He didn't have to ask it; we were going to buy the furniture anyway, but most likely the wrong size. In the end, because Bart asked this question, we were the ones who took action without his having to ask us to buy. I believe in finding out and matching the customers' wants/needs/desires with the products and services you have. This way, everyone comes out a winner.

Lemon Aid Links: Win/Win/Win

Abundance Attitude

Perhaps you've heard that you must have a Positive Mental Attitude to succeed in life. I believe this is true, but this isn't the only kind of attitude you need to cultivate success. I also believe you must possess certain other mindsets. One of these mindsets is to have an **Abundance Attitude.**

I have seen many people fail in their business ventures because they believed the only people they could service and sell to were their "warm" market of family and friends. Once that market had been exhausted (it doesn't take long), they threw in the towel and blamed the business failure on not having any customers. This was the premise I used in writing **The Lemon Aid Lead Alphabet: Where to Find Customers when you run out of Family and Friends**. Before you go any further in this book, read the **Lead Alphabet** if you haven't done so yet. Because if you have read and practiced the information in the **Lead Alphabet**, you should now have an *overabundance of leads* and are probably wondering what to do with them. In fact, you'll have such an *abundance*, your next challenge will be to keep up with all of the follow through and profits! This is a *good* problem!

You create an Abundance Attitude by opening your eyes to bigger landscapes and seeing beyond the horizon to realize there is enough business for all who are willing to work and persevere.

People fail in their pursuits because they become afraid of competition—they believe that others will encroach upon their hard-earned business.

So, before you read on in this book, open your eyes. Think of the millions of people—literally—that you can sell to and service.

Your family and friends will constantly remind you that you'll soon run out of business—DON'T LISTEN TO THEM!! Just *prove them wrong* by keeping your Abundance Attitude; the world is full of buyers and sellers. You only need *a small portion* of the huge population to become successful and wealthy.

Answering Devices

Setting the rings. Have your answering machine turn on after three or four rings. If you cannot answer the phone within this amount of rings, you are probably not prepared to do business anyway and should let the machine take over. If the rings are set too high (over four), the potential customer might hang up before the machine turns on.

Business Line. On your answering machine or voice mail, record a message that will leave the caller feeling great that they called you. **Be happy and sound excited on your recording!!** Tell them who they've reached, what you have to offer, and, if appropriate, when you'll be available to answer their call.

Some **words you might choose**:

"It's a great day here at the _____(company name) office of _____(your name)! Please leave your name and phone number so I can tell you all about _____(current specials/promotions—be to the point, but get their attention!)" If you have a personalized slogan, add it to your message to reinforce the mission of your business.

Your lead might have called to ask a question about the use and care of a product but will now want more information about the special promotion you mentioned in your message. This will increase your sales, profits, business, and give more value to your customer's call—and costs you virtually nothing!!

Adding a **commercial for recruiting/hiring** is very effective.

"I am adding two energetic people to my team this week; one could be YOU!"

If you'll be away from your office for an extended period of time, and cannot or do not want to remotely retrieve messages, inform the caller of your absence and when to expect a return call.

"I'll be out of my office until _____ "
This way the caller won't think you haven't received the call or feel neglected when you haven't returned the call right away. Give yourself some leeway--especially if you'll be gone for an extended period. If you'll be returning Monday morning, say you'll return the call by Tuesday at noon. This way, if you have a lot of calls, you will have ample time to return them by the promised deadline. People usually like to be surprised when you're early rather than upset if you're late!

On your **home line**, record a regular message, but add a brief business commercial:

Sample: Thank you for calling the _____ family (or for calling _____ [your phone number]). If you want a return call, please leave your name and phone number. If you're calling to buy or sell _____ products, indicate that on your message.

Or change the last line to:

"If you're calling to buy or sell _____ products, please indicate that on your message and yours will be the first call returned!"

You never know who might be calling your home who DOESN'T know you have a business. Perhaps the mother of one of your kid's friends, a business associate of your spouse, a doctor's office reminding you of an appointment, etc. If you have a separate business line, refer callers to that number where they will hear your detailed commercial.

Call your own phone numbers every couple of weeks to hear what your callers hear when they call. Keep your messages updated and enthusiastic!

Lemon Aid Links: Return Phone Calls, Telephone Tips, Voice Mail

Lemon Aid Lead Alphabet: Telephone

Anniversaries

For a TWIST that will give you and your business attention, recognize the anniversary of when you met and began business with a customer, hostess, or recruit. Or, send cards on their wedding anniversary.   Send these greetings via mail or e-mail and include a gift offer in celebration of the anniversary.

For people you don't know yet and want to do business with, use wedding sections of the newspaper to send congratulations on silver and golden anniversaries (the milestones usually announced).   I suggest sending a card with your business card enclosed—no other advertising.   Within two weeks, make a personal phone call to introduce yourself over the phone and continue with the follow-through ideas you'll read in the rest of this book.

File the wedding section after using it to send these anniversary greetings to contact newlyweds—after the honeymoon. Even though anniversary means "annual", most newlyweds celebrate their union by months until their first anniversary (just like new mothers!). Create a 3-6-9 or 12-month celebration by sending congratulations. Send only greetings with your business card, not advertising.

An idea for following through here is to ask if they received any of your product as a gift that needs to be exchanged. Most will have not; however, they are impressed that you asked and will usually be very open to your sales and service.

Lemon Aid Links: E-mail, Get to Know You Cards, Internet

Lemon Aid Lead Alphabet: Newspaper

Appearance

Referring to beauty, you've probably heard "it's what's inside that counts." This is a true statement about *beauty,* but it doesn't apply to *appearance* in general. The way you are groomed and dressed <u>does</u> count when you are on a sales call, doing a group presentation, or anytime you meet with a customer. If you feel you're not a magazine-cover beauty (not many of us are), that's okay. You can still attract people to do business with you because you are clean, well groomed, and in your own way, beautiful.

As elementary as this seems, be sure to use deodorant every day (more than once if you're running around a lot and each time you change clothes), brush your teeth (use breath mints if necessary), comb your hair, and be sure your clothes are clean and neatly pressed. Shined and cleaned shoes as well as manicured fingernails add to your overall polished appearance. If you spend a lot of time in your car going from appointment to appointment, keep a kit filled with mints, comb, hairspray, toothbrush and toothpaste. Women should add makeup for touch ups, and even an extra pair of hose.

Appropriate Dress. Each company and industry has written and unwritten dress codes for appropriate dress. My rule of thumb is to dress as if I am going on a job interview, keeping in mind my interviewers (audience). If my audience is professional people whom I know will come to the presentation in business attire, I will dress in a similar way. If I am presenting to a neighborhood group at a local park, I dress down a bit, but always a step up from what my audience wears. Even though I know they'll be in shorts and T-shirts, I wear nice pant suits or a casual dress. You can always get more casual (by removing your tie or jacket, rolling up your sleeves, etc.), but dressing up after you arrive at a presentation or sales call is difficult. One consultant told me that she looks in a full-length mirror before leaving her house and asks herself, "Would I do business with me?"--very good retrospective question.

Unfortunately, I've seen many people with enthusiasm and knowledge of their product and plan who distract customers because they lack attention to their personal appearance. My first impression of a home-based business salesperson was marred when I attended a presentation over 20 years ago. The presenter looked and acted as if she had been home all day chasing her kids; she was exhausted! Her clothes were stretch pants and a t-shirt, both of which were too tight. I didn't choose to do further business with her because of her lack of personal grooming, although I do remember she shared some great ideas in the presentation. Subconsciously, prospective customers and recruits wonder if you don't take care of yourself, how would you take care of their needs.

Conversely, I have a friend who dressed for business even if she just ran a quick errand, and always when meeting with customers. One of the conventions she attended was within driving distance of her home—about six hours. To be comfortable in the car, she wore a pair of sweats and a sweat shirt. When she checked in to the hotel, her co-workers were shocked to see her in pants—let alone sweats! She said she learned a valuable lesson about the impact of dressing professionally whenever representing her company.

The appearance of your product, demonstration kit, and sales literature is also very important. These items all reflect your overall attitude of how you do business and what you think of yourself. Be very careful that these items are clean and, if you recycle nearly-new, gently-used literature like I do, check to be sure they do not have any signs of having been used by someone else.

At the same presentation I mentioned earlier, the presenter told how she had to take food out of the containers to bring to the presentation that evening. Her items were scratched and stained and even had food odor. I didn't order anything from that presentation because I really thought she might use my products before she gave them to me!

As our discussion of how to attract customers by attractive appearance ends, I will share a good example. Recently, I was driving to another state to speak at some seminars. While driving through Albuquerque, New Mexico, the tire on my car looked really low. My husband suggested we get it checked out, and we ended up at Discount Tire.

I rarely go to tire stores; usually that is in my husband's job description. I don't like being around greasy, dirty car shops. However, I was in for a surprise. While sitting in the very clean waiting room, I noticed all of the men who were servicing customers were really clean and very well groomed, as well as polite. By coincidence, I was doing the final editing of this book, right in this section on appearance. I was so impressed by the physical appearance of both the tire store and the employees, I just had to make mention of it. If a place that is usually known for not being neat and clean can attract a customer like me, I know all of us can use our appearance to convert leads to customers. Added to this, we were not charged for the repair! What great customer service! When we arrived at our destination, we met our son. He told us his car needed new tires, and of course we referred him to the local Discount Tire company, where he also had a pleasant experience.

Lemon Aid Links: Packaging and Perception, Service

Appreciation to Customers

You will save time and money retaining your customers rather than putting all your efforts into getting new ones. As you please your current customers, they will spread the word and tell their family and friends about you. One key to customer retention is *appreciation..*

How do you show appreciation? The first way is by thanking customers for doing business with you. Verbal thanks are expected, and most people do this out of habit **Thank you notes** are my favorite way to be shown appreciation as a customer and to show appreciation to my customers. If you want to demonstrate sincere thanks, and to be remembered as "their" service provider, a tangible, hand-written note is best. The note stands apart from the daily barrage of bills and/or junk mail; many times I've seen the notes I've sent displayed in my customers' homes and offices. As you start your business, written thank you notes don't take a lot of time as you are just building your customer base and don't have that many customers.

Then a **follow-up phone call** after they've used your product/service for a while is really effective. Not only are you taking the time to see if they are pleased with their purchase, but you can thank them again for the order, and then ask for future business and referrals.

Depending on how many orders you receive in a week, sending a personal written thank you note to every single person who purchases from you might not be feasible. However, you can use "Thank You for your Order" stickers from The Booster (1-800-5JENNYB) on the order form--this shows you took a little extra effort to show thanks. The Booster also has a variety of Thank You postcards. A hand-written one- or two-line message can be added to these postcards, and it costs less to mail than a letter. At the very least, pre-printed, mass-produced thank you notes show some appreciation and take little effort. Sending these out within five to fifteen days after purchase or delivery is a good time frame for follow through.

Thank you gifts serve two purposes: First, as a token of appreciation for business, and second, as a way for the customer to remember you and your superb service so they'll become residual customers who refer their family and friends to you.

Gifts priced relative to the cost of the product/service purchased--as well as to your profit margin--are a nice touch when you feel they are appropriate. Real Estate Agents are known for sending housewarming gifts to new home owners. Gifts should be personalized as much as possible and be chosen appropriately for the customer. Use the "Getting to Know You" cards for ideas. Use particular care in giving food gifts as well as alcoholic beverages since people often have restricted diets, health concerns, and religious beliefs associated with these items. The best gifts are items that somehow compliment the product that was purchased. If appropriate, put your name and phone number somewhere on the gift (the bottom of a nice figurine, for example) so when your customers need to contact you with referrals, they will have easy access to your information. Labels work well for this use. But, remember, most people would love to receive a personal, hand written thank you rather than a meaningless gift they can't use.

Over the past several months, I have purchased a newly-built home, an expensive computer system, a refrigerator, and a vacuum cleaner. The house and vacuum cleaner were purchased from sales people who work on a commission basis--they really depend on repeat customers! The computer system and refrigerator were purchased from a local retail establishment. I didn't receive any kind of thank you from the purchase of any of these items. However, the employees of the retail store (Best Buy in Lewisville, Texas--Store Manager Tom Frost) have given me much better service and taken care of my after-the-sale needs than the two people who worked on commission. Who will I give referrals to? Not the commissioned sales people. And, in the case of the vacuum, I helped the sales person meet his monthly sales goal so he could win a contest. But, I didn't even get an acknowledgement of the sale besides the obligatory verbal thank you as he was leaving my home.

Where to purchase gifts. If your company doesn't provide vendors with items at special prices, look at your customer base. Could one of your customers become one of your vendors? I believe in doing business with those who do business with me. The more business you give your customers, the more money they'll have to do more business with you! You might both consider a barter arrangement as well.

Lemon Aid Links: Getting to Know You
Lead Alphabet: Barter

Autographs

Here's a tried and true way to add value to your materials as well as to encourage and reward leads to keep your information, thus eliminating waste. As a sales professional, you will have your personal NAPEF (name, address {in some cases}, phone, e-mail, fax) printed, stamped, or stickered on all your sales literature. Go a step beyond what everyone else does.

Autograph your sales literature/catalog/business cards etc., Don't just have pre-signed items. Autograph and customize the information with your lead's name while he/she is watching you. An added benefit to writing the name is you will have a better chance of remembering it. The lead also feels more special. Tell him/her how lucky she/he is to have your autograph. Adding a sticker that says "autographed copy" adds even more worth—you can get these stickers from The Booster at 1-800-5JENNYB.

If you sell your products/service through group presentations, you can encourage repeat attendance and more new presentations with these autographed items. As I close my presentation, I announce I'd love to autograph their book (catalog, literature, etc.). After they have collected three of my autographs at three separate events, I will have a gift for them. An idea for this unique gift is a special Booster magnet with my name and/or business card attached. This way, the customer has a more permanent souvenir with your NAPEF. When I promoted this, I was amazed at how the guests would decide among themselves who would do the next two presentations so they could all collect my autographs and get the gift!

When you write a check at the store, intentionally leave your signature off. As the cashier looks over the check he/she will remind you that you need to sign it. Apologize for the oversight, then say, "I forgot to autograph my check?....Would you like a book (business card, flyer, etc) with my autograph for you to keep?" As you promote your autograph, your fame will really spread! Who knows how much your autograph will be worth some day!

Autographed copies of books are always more valuable and personal (is this book personally autographed by me? If not, send it to my office; I'll sign and return it).

Let's *TWIST* this concept to when taking orders or enrolling people in our organizations. Rather than saying, "Will you please **sign** this order/form?" Treat the customer like a celebrity. You could say, "Once I have your **autograph**, your order will be on its way." When you ask for a **signature,** it seems so "legal"— sometimes people are even skeptical of "signing" anything. However the term **autograph** sounds warm, friendly, and pleasurable.

Lemon Aid Links: Literature, Positioning and Promoting

Awards

Award customers for purchasing a certain number of units of your products, or for having a specified amount of orders in an established time period. These awards can be in the form of gift certificates or complimentary products. In addition to the gift certificate or gift, create an award certificate they can keep as a remembrance.

You can also design awards specific to your customer. When someone has the **largest order** you've ever taken, create an award certificate for him/her. Who has given you **the most orders?** Which customer has given you the **most referrals**, the **most referrals who became customers**? Do you have a long-distance **customer who orders every month?**

Lemon Aid Links: Appreciation, Files, Frequent Buyers

MY OWN DEED IDEAS:

<u>B</u>

Benefits

You've had this happen before. A salesperson calls you on the phone or meets you in person. She goes on and on about the features of the product/service she has to offer. As she rambles, you tune her out because you don't see the connection between her product's features and what you need or want.

I have a great tool **I want** to sell you. Here are all the features: "The ends are rounded, it is lightweight, inexpensive, and attracted to magnets. Papers can be held together tightly." When you read this, what are you thinking? Are you saying, "So What? Why do I care?"

Let's do the *TWIST* and relate the features of a product to the benefits **you need:** Do you have a problem with a messy desk? Have you ever lost an important document because it was mixed in with piles of papers? Here is a great new tool that will help you get more organized and productive: The Paper Clip! This magnificent tool has a unique shape that will hold stacks of papers together **so** you don't lose important documents. The paper clip is lightweight **so that** your papers won't bend when they are held in place. You won't get pinched by the paper clip **because** its ends are smooth and round. Paper clips are easy to store **because** they are attracted to magnets. Keep a magnet in your drawer or on your desk, put the paper clips on the magnet, and they won't move. If you have stacks of papers that need to be sorted and organized, you'll be able to afford to buy boxes **because** paper clips cost less than a penny a piece!"

If you find yourself simply *listing* information, you are probably having a monologue about features. However, if you list and feature and bridge it with, "so", "so that", or "because" you are linking the features to the benefits for the customer and can show how the product will solve a problem. Don't let the lead be thinking, "so what?," but explain "so that" and "because."

Features tell, but benefits sell!! Adapt the features to each person's needs. The potential customer is silently saying: "Show me the **benefits**, and I'll show you the **money**!" Convert the features in to benefits, and you'll convert a lead into a customer! Lemon Aid Links: dialogues and monologues, word pictures

Birthdays

Most companies throw special sales because of their own birthdays or anniversary. Put a *TWIST* on this idea: **celebrate the customer, not your business.**

Call people who have birthdays this month. Tell them you want to celebrate THEM.

You can:
- give a discount on your products.
- give a free product; something extra in your inventory is a good choice.
- schedule a demonstration with the birthday person so you can present them with the gift item .
- throw a party for the birthday person with your products if your product is sold through presentations! A nice gesture is to bring the refreshments or the ingredients for dessert if your company does food demonstration classes.
- throw a surprise party. Call one of their closest friends and schedule the demonstration for your product. Have the friend invite the birthday person's friends and relatives to the demonstration. When the birthday person arrives, shout SURPRISE. All the gifts from the sales and new demonstrations scheduled will go to the birthday person!
- hold a Birthday Bash each month and invite all customers with birthdays in that month. Have a token gift for each person as well as special sales or gift certificates toward their purchases.

- Send a birthday card if nothing else. They will remember you for remembering them. Include a gift certificate for their next purchase valid for 30 days following their birthday if you want to encourage a purchase.

How do you know when their birthday is? ASK. If they filled out an information form to receive your product or service, it might be on there. If not, use a "Getting to Know you" form. Keep a large calendar or use a page in your appointment book just for birthdays. Keep these separate from your daily calendar to avoid confusion.

Lemon Aid Links: Getting to Know You

Birthday Club

To find out if your customer wants to be honored on his/her birthday, invite him/her to sign up for your Birthday Club. You can simply use 3 x 5 index cards and put the information on your Birthday Calendar. As you convert leads to customers, notify them of this special recognition you offer. This way, the customers who want to be honored will register.

Birthday Club for Kids. If you sell a child-related product (toys, books, etc), begin a Birthday Club for Kids. When new customers purchase your product, have them fill out a form listing their child's/children's birthday(s). Purchase inexpensive birthday cards or have some printed. Enclose a coupon for dollars or a percentage off the next purchase valid for 30 days from the birthday. Kids love getting the cards, and parents love the discount. This also gives the parents great gift-giving ideas. Be sure to mail out a few weeks in advance to allow for birthday delivery. As with any method of selling, a phone call following through on the mailing will increase your response rate.

Lemon Aid Links: Birthdays, Getting to Know You

Business Bank

In the course of your business, you'll meet **people who want to do business with you at a later date**. You deposit their information in a safe place for future retrieval, just like money in a bank. This is my version of what high tech calls contact management. The idea is to keep track of when to call customers and to keep records of those contacts. I prefer to call this a business bank because bank represents the bottom line: profits! So, I'll teach you how to do this with your hard-copy calendar system. You can transfer this information to your computer if you choose.

1. In the **appointment schedule system** that you are using, find a place in your planner or calendar organizer just for your Business Bank.
2. Have at least one page for every month of the year, starting with the month you are in currently. Label the pages by month. If today is March, begin with April and go through to the next March. You'll always have at least12 pages in your business bank just like the 12 months of the year. You can have more than one page per month if you have that many names to put on the pages.
3. Have columns for writing the person's name, address, phone, where you met the person, and any personal notes.

Here's a scenario: I've just met a potential customer/hostess, Ruth, and she tells me, "I'd love to purchase your products/have a demonstration, but my son is graduating from college in May, and my daughter is getting married in June." I *ask her* (this is the key) when she wants me to call her. The reason for asking—not assuming—is that whenever I've assumed a time, I found the customer usually prefers me to call sooner. And, as the saying goes, the sooner the better!

Ruth tells me to call her in July. How do I keep track of this information? Do I go to my July calendar and find a place to put her name? Absolutely not! My calendar gets really messy, and if I randomly write in something as important as this, chances are I'd lose her number and name among everything else I've written! Instead, I go to the July page of my Business Bank and write down her NAPEF <u>and</u> note the wedding and graduation.

July is coming up. I turn to the July page of my Business Bank and see Ruth's name, and I call her. What is the first thing I ask? I ask how the wedding and graduation went. This develops rapport and builds a business relationship. She'll be amazed that I called her exactly when *she requested* and that I remembered about the graduation and wedding.

In this phone call, Ruth tells me that her husband surprised her with a European cruise this month, and July, after all, will not be a good time to purchase my product/have a demonstration. Do I act disappointed? Of course not, I'm thrilled for her. So, I *ask* her when she'd like me to call back. She tells me to call her in September. Now I move her information to September and make a note about the European cruise. When September comes, I go through the same process.

How many times do you put customers in your business bank? Sometimes I've contacted people for more than a year before any business was transacted. After the third call, I am very frank. When they ask me to call them back—again—I promise to do so as long as they acknowledge that I am not bothering them. This gives them an out if they are just being polite. Most people really do want you to continue to contact them.

Calling before the requested time. Sometimes I'll have someone in my Business Bank who asks me to call in the fall. However, in July a new promotion is announced that I *know* this person would *love*. Do I wait? NO. I call her but with a different approach. I'd suggest something like "Jill, I know I promised that I'd call you in September, (you're acknowledging your agreement) but I just heard some news that I thought you'd be interested in." By stating that September is when I am really supposed to call, she recognized that I am being considerate, but also wanting to help her .

Use this deposit system whenever you are talking to and meeting new customers, at or away from demonstrations, or when doing follow up calls. This is a very simple, profitable system. I think of this business bank as if it were my money bank. I always want to be making deposits so that I can always make withdrawals.

Every six months, take the previous months' Business Banks and file or place in a binder. You can always go back and see who you called from your business bank in the past. Contact those people who never did business with you. They might have changed their minds or their situations might make doing business more appealing. I never throw NAPEFs away; they are worth thousands of dollars—and more!

Business Card Magnets

You can have your cards professionally printed on magnets or simply mount your business cards on a magnet sheets purchased at craft stores using rubber cement. Most people love magnets for hanging notes on their fridge. They'll surely keep this and think of you every time they open their refrigerator. Give these "collectible magnets" when you first meet a lead. When you do the follow through, the person will already be familiar with you because your magnet has been on display.

If you go door-to-door to meet new customers or delivery flyers about your business, use the magnet to hang the literature on front doors if the doors are made of steel—most new homes have this type of door. The first time I did this, I had customers calling me before I got back home!

Lemon Aid Links: Magnets

Lead Alphabet: Door-to-Door, those you'd like to know

MY OWN DEED IDEAS:

C

Calendars

Calendars, in many forms, can help you convert a lead to a long-time customer. Send a monthly or quarterly calendar to the leads on your list giving information on special prices, spotlighted products, and educational/entertaining events to attend. When the lead sees an item or event that is of interest, he will take action. In my business of holding sales seminars, I find my customers like to know my calendar in advance so they can attend a seminar at their convenience. Your calendar can be included as part of a newsletter. Remind the lead to write in all celebration and special occasion days such as birthdays, anniversaries, wedding, etc. Add gift suggestions for these occasions. Your gift sales will begin to increase as the leads become aware of your product as a gift.

You can also create a calendar to be given out at the beginning of each year. Many ad specialty companies have these available and will print your company name, phone and address. This way, customers have your information available all year and think of you when they refer to their calendar. Purchase colorful stickers to put on important dates. Some of the Booster (l-800-5JENNYB) stickers will help to remind them to call you with orders for gift giving occasions, to schedule a demonstration, etc. These colorful visuals will be a boost to your sales.

Printing a small calendar on the back of your business card also adds value and encourages the customer to keep your business card—preferably in their wallet where they will see your name often and do business with you on a regular basis.

Lemon Aid Links: Educational and Entertaining Events, Newsletters

Celebrations

Watch for reasons to celebrate your customer. Is this month a birthday or anniversary for her? Was she recently married? Is she a new mother? Did she celebrate a milestone anniversary? Was she recently promoted in her career? Does she have a new home? Did a member of her family excel in something (child on honor roll, scholarship awarded, military service, etc.)?

Where do you get this information? Every time you talk to your customer, ask questions about her life. Not only will you discover these celebrations, you'll find more ways of servicing her. Sometimes the reason she/he cannot do business with you right now is one of these celebrations (new baby, new job, etc.).

Even if an event happened months before, send a congratulatory note. She'll realize you just found out about the event. Other ways to find celebration reasons are when you are talking to her friends, reading the local paper, and referring to the "Getting to Know you" card. This contact of celebrations cements the relationship you have with this customer. Capitalize on what you learn about the customer and the celebrations in her/his life.

Lemon Aid Links: Birthdays, Getting to Know You
Lead Alphabet Book - Newspapers

Checking Back

After customers have had/used your product/service for a while, check back to see how they are enjoying it. If they are having problems, take care of the situation. Most of the time problems result because the customer needs guidance in using the product. This is an opportune time to teach tips. Being proactive will demonstrate you are focused not only on selling but more importantly on solving problems and servicing your customers. This also verifies the belief you have in your product and service. You're not afraid to call back and see the customer is more than satisfied.

How do you check back? I start out with a postcard that simply expresses my thanks and add a quick, personalized note. This is mailed five to fifteen days after I know they have the product. This allows them time to use the product/service and discover any questions/problems they have.

A week or two after they would have received this postcard, I randomly choose customers to call. Because of the volume of business you'll be doing, you would have to hire someone to do these calls if you wanted to contact everyone, which might be a good idea.

The first question I ask (after I'm sure this is a good time to chat) is, "Do you love your _____?" I realize this is a very close-ended question and requires a yes or no. This is what you'll need to ask so you can get right to the point, and you'll be able to tell their true feelings this way. If they are happy with what has been ordered, offer complimenting products that would enhance the use of what they have. You can take their order right then, or see if they'd like to schedule a demonstration or become a consultant.

Perhaps they are happy with the product but the options listed above are not of interest to them. Ask for referrals. The best approach is to **say something like:**

"Who do you know who would be as thrilled about this item as you are?" Or, "Since you've been using _____ who have you shown it to?"

Lemon Aid Links: Complementing products, Set$

Coming Attractions

What are some easy ways for customers to remember your name? How do you remember theirs? What is the most important tool in planning a successful group presentation?   What are "Profitiles?" Are you using them to increase your business?

Have I captured your attention and interest? You are reading only the first third of this book, and yet I'm already telling you about a future Lemon Aid Book: Pre$entation$ 4 Profit.

When you go to the movies, the first thing you see when the lights are dimmed are the previews of coming attractions. The movie makers want you to come back. You want your customers to feel the same way. **Let them know you have more to offer - leave them wanting more and more!**

Promote a product or theme of the month and sprinkle "teasers" about coming attractions throughout your conversation and/or demonstration.

Communication - Good News

Communication is Motivation and Motivation is Communication.. If you want to motivate your leads to do business with you, communicate with them! You'll find several sections in this book to help meet this goal.

Your communications with a customer could be on a product they've expressed an interest in, an event that is coming up, or just monthly, bimonthly, or semi-annual announcements. Perhaps you have customers who want to be notified whenever new products are available or a new catalog is released. As a salesperson, you need to begin the communication process and keep it moving—keep customers motivated with your communication!

Lemon Aid Links: Appreciation, Contact on a Regular Basis, E-mail, Fax, Internet, Telephone Tips

Communication - Not So Good News

Sometimes you'll have to communicate bad news, such as late deliveries, back ordered products, wrong item/color shipped, sale is over, etc. Better to tell the prospect this news than have him discover it himself and be upset.

If you can deliver bad news in a positive way, the customer will probably be fine. In this case, give your customers the 3 C's: communication - choice -compensation.

Communication: When I was a teenager, my parents didn't mind if I came in a little bit late, as long as I called them and explained where I was and when I would be home. If I didn't call, they became worried and upset. If you have some not-so-good news for customers, don't let them sit and wonder what is going on—inform them. Because they are notified, they are usually not upset. Nonetheless, give them a choice as to what they want to do in light of the situation…

Choice: Now that the situation has taken a TWIST, give the customer another option and let him/her make the choice best suited to their needs. For example, if the product is in a back order situation, offer to refund the money or deliver the item as soon as it is available. Most people will wait, now that they've been informed, and are more likely to do so when you offer additional compensation…

Compensation: Because the customer might have been inconvenienced due to the change in plans, give a token of compensation to retain goodwill—regardless of the customers' choice in the matter. This token does not have to be expensive; the gesture, however, can be invaluable in retaining residual customers and profits.

Communicate delivery dates, schedules, policies, and other information pertinent to the transaction. During a rather lengthy car trip, I checked into a hotel for the night. Because I had been driving all day, I was anxious to have a nourishing dinner and then spend some time relaxing in the hot tub. I was impressed that the hotel had a map and listing of the closest restaurants, theatres, and shopping locations—better than most I've seen in hotels. This information assisted our family in driving in the right direction to find a restaurant.

When we returned to the room, at about 10 p.m., we dressed in our bathing suits in anticipation of relaxing in the hot tub. As I looked for information on the hotel regarding hours of the pool and hot tub, none were found. Since most hotels I've stayed in have the pool facilities open until 11 p.m., we made our way to the hot tub. The gate was locked; no signs or information were posted regarding any hours. We went to the front desk, and the clerk told us the pool and hot tub closed at 10:00.

All day I had been looking forward to chilling out in the warm water—now my bubble was burst. Had I seen signs or read information alerting me of the hours, I would have understood. Now, however, I was a little upset. The clerk was a bit defensive at first, and then I could tell she shifted from having a conversation with another person to the role of a customer service agent. She kindly apologized and explained the early closing was due to insurance liability. She asked what I would like her to do. My response: I want a hot tub! I was hoping the hotel would have had vacancies in a room with a whirlpool, but they did not. Even though I did not have much of a choice in how I wanted this matter resolved, the clerk did offer compensation in the way of a reduced room rate. At this point, I probably would have *paid more money* to have a hot tub, but I did appreciate the gesture of good will and willingness to keep a customer. I will return to that hotel and tell others to do so as well.

Lemon Aid Link: Service

Competition

Your competitors can help you grow your business--and you can help them, as well, which turns into more leads, more customers, more profits for everyone.

First, identify who your competition is. Are your competitors people who are selling the same product for the same company (coworkers), a similar product for another company, or a different product with the same type of plan/organization? In reality, **your competitor is anyone who vies for your customers' attention and money.**

How can you learn from them so everyone has more customers and more profits? If they are coworkers, the best thing you can do is encourage them to grow their own businesses. The more you do, the more they are out in the marketplace telling the world about your product. When you meet someone, they might have heard about your product from this coworker, but were not able or willing to purchase at that time. Now, upon meeting you, they have been primed for the product and are willing to purchase because they have already heard about it from your coworker. Always build others, they will build your business. When you befriend and help your coworkers, they respect you, ask your assistance, and consider you an expert. Be happy for everyone's successes, and you'll have more personal successes to be happy about.

If circumstances ever change and they leave the business, you have a right and obligation to ask for their customer records. Because you have created a good relationship with them, they are often willing to pass the information along. You can even offer to give them a one-time bonus for business you generate. Additionally, now that they no longer represent your same product, they become a very loyal customer rather than coworker.

Other competitors with similar products/plans. First, find out what they are all about. How do you do this? Attend their functions, visit their stores. Sam Walton was an expert at this. He was always stopping in at the stores of his competition to see what he could learn. And, that is the idea. Not to find "secrets" or faults, but to see what they are doing and how you can *TWIST* this information into growing your own business. If you sell your product on a presentation plan, attend the presentations of other companies. See what is working for them, and what doesn't appear to be, then *TWIST* this information to your benefit. However, do not try to take away or influence the customers/guests who are there to do business with your competitors. That is not only bad manners but dishonest business ethics as well.

Lastly, you need to know your competitors' products and how they compare to yours. This way, when a customer comes to you with these comparisons, you'll be informed. NEVER, EVER degrade or put down someone else or their product. This only lowers your reputation in the eyes of the customer and makes you look bitter. When you acknowledge you know about the features of a competing product/plan, you add value in the eyes of the customer. She knows you are serious enough about your product/industry to have investigated the rest and have decided to work with the best product/plan for you.

You might find that your product will not serve a customer as well as a competitor's. If you refer the customer elsewhere, she trusts you more because of your integrity and will do business with and refer business to you, as will the competitor when *your product* would work *better than what he has to offer.* Become friends with competing coworkers and suppliers, network together, realize the world has an abundance for everyone when we all work hard and share!

Lemon Aid Links: Abundance Mentality, Knowledge, Miracle on 34th Street

Lead Alphabet: Former Customers

Complaints

Complaints are a part of doing business. Complaints actually help you improve your product and service because you find out what the customers like and don't like. How you handle these "sour situations" will determine what kinds of "sweet successes and juicy profits" you'll experience.

Complaints cover two areas: your service and your product. While you might not have total control over the tangible product you sell, normally you're in charge of the type of service you provide. As hard as you try, you won't please everybody all of the time. So, I suggest you live the golden rule and move up to the platinum rule: Treat others how *you would like* to be treated; find out their needs and then treat them how *they want* to be treated. If you make an error in your attempt to provide quality service and you hear complaints, graciously (key word) learn from them. Complaints are recommendations for improvement in disguise. If you handle complaints in a professional manner, you should be able to restore the goodwill of your customer.

I believe in compensation for complaints—even if the complaints are not always valid. Offer to redo the work, give the product for free or a reduced fee, and so forth. I know many people are in the complaining business—that's their unofficial job. Do your best to satisfy their needs and "kill 'em with kindness." While you want to have all customers happy, this usually doesn't happen. Accept this fact. The complainer will go elsewhere (luckily for you) and you'll go on giving superb service to the other 99.9% of your customers. Never make decisions based on the sour attitude of one person.

A devastated business owner e-mailed me because a customer's check bounced and she wanted some guidance. She decided that she would no longer accept personal checks because she had been burned. She actually had a great track record. She had been in business for a couple years and this was the first returned check! I envied her record! I suggested she not penalize the honest people by continuing to accept their checks—perhaps with a *TWIST*, such as waiting to ship product till the check clears.

If the complaint is about your company's product, politely listen to the complaint yourself or lead the customer in the direction of getting the complaint resolved. Each company has its own policies and procedures. When I have a problem with a purchase or service as a consumer, I prefer to call the person at the company who I know—the salesperson who benefited from my purchase—"customer service" is a department who doesn't really know who I am! One of my pet peeves is to be tossed from one person to the next trying to get my complaint solved! Sometimes I feel like the company didn't mind taking my money, but now that I have a problem, I've become a burden! As a salesperson, I want to know if my customers have a problem; not only for this transaction but for future business.   If I have an unhappy customer, and I don't know it because all complaints go to customer service, when I call the customer the next time and he/she is cold or upset, I'll feel like I'm in the dark. I might actually lose a customer because I was not informed about the situation.   If your company does have a customer service department, tell your customers to call you first so you're aware of the situation. Then you can direct them to the correct person to get the situation resolved. Call the customer back later that day to be sure everything is okay. This restores goodwill and retains customers.

In any case, NEVER TELL the customer he/she caused the problem. (even if you know it was!). This puts everyone on the defensive, and everyone loses. Instead, use passive language:

"The staples weren't inserted correctly." Rather than, "You put the staples in wrong!" This softens the blow and keeps the conversation neutral rather than pointing fingers..

 I've found that when the customer has done damage to the product, it is due to lack of education. This is the perfect time to suggest the customer attend/host a presentation or educational/entertaining event to learn the proper use and care.

Never tell the customer that they are the only one who had this problem--they feel guilty and at fault even if they are not. I had someone tell me, "Well, I'll go ahead and have it fixed (the item was under full warranty), but we've never seen this happen before!" I felt like I was being told, "No one has been this stupid before, but we'll do what we can--if we can!"

Lemon Aid Links: Kindness, Requests

Complementing Products

As you are taking a customer's order, notice the items being purchased. Do you have an item that would really enhance the products being ordered? For example, if you sell candles and the order has several candles, but no candle holders, show the benefits of using the holders. Or, vice versa, the customer might buy the candle holder and not realize she needs to buy a candle to go in it. Most catalogs show items grouped together, but sometimes the items are ordered separately. Educate your leads on this so when the order is delivered, they won't be disappointed or mad. And, if this does happen, don't be defensive and say, "I told you the candles didn't come with the holder!" Keep a customer! Think about these things ahead of time by being observant.

Keep track of what products your customers purchase, so when you are doing call backs, you can offer suggestions for additional products/services that would enhance the use of what they already have. Filing order forms is a good way to keep track of this information. These suggestions might be newly-released products or an extension of the item they already have. If the customer raves about the product and gives you new ideas for using it, suggest she order more items for herself.

Lemon Aid Links: Files. multiples, Set$

Complimentary Samples

This is another word for free samples, but "complimentary" sounds classier than "free"! If your product is one that customers can sample small amounts of, use this concept to your benefit.

I recently heard of a new business, Tastefully Simple. One of the consultants, Eileen Robbins, had purchased The Lemon Aid Lead Alphabet and called me with some questions. Since I hadn't heard about her product or company, she offered to send me some information, and she included a sample of a spinach dip mix.

I immediately had to try it, and loved it! Receiving this complimentary sample encouraged me to take action and purchase more of the real thing!

If you sell pianos, giving a sample of the ivories could be difficult. Why not do a *TWIST* and give a complimentary cassette tape or CD with someone playing the piano? Weekenders Clothing gives sample color swatches; Story Tellers gives samples of the felt fabric that their products are printed on. Touching, tasting, and using a product encourages purchasing!

Contact on a Regular Basis

Keeping in touch with customers on a regular basis shows you really care about helping them. You position yourself not only as a salesperson, but more importantly in the eyes of your customers, a knowledgeable resource person who knows the business. Contact can be done on a monthly, quarterly, or semi-annually basis. I would suggest twice yearly as a minimum. Of course as your customer base expands, you probably won't get to do this with every single person. However, you know those customers who want to continue to do business with you. The ones who are the most interested in your product/service, those who order more than once, those who attend or host demonstrations, and especially those you have created a relationship with.

Lemon Aid Links: Calendar, Checking back, Communication, Newsletter, Internet

Coupons Because You're a Customer

Finding new customers by offering a special coupon is a good idea, but I suggest you do a *TWIST* on this idea and offer established customers a coupon for being loyal. I get upset when an establishment I regularly patronize offers discounts or premiums for new customers only. This excludes the loyal patrons, and I look elsewhere so I can be "new" to another service person. Always treat your current customers the best and give them special treatment. Of course, you can give incentives to get new business, but if a current customer comes in with the offer or coupon, by all means honor it! Never penalize a customer for being loyal.

Courting Customers

After Follow Through, this section is the next most important part of this book. Have you been or are you involved in the dating scene? Thankfully I've been happily married for over 22 years, so I don't have to worry about trying to impress anyone anymore, right? Absolutely wrong!! The person I need to impress the most is my best friend and husband--Bob!! Just because we wear wedding rings and have been legally married doesn't mean we'll live happily ever after. My husband and I continue to do things to strengthen our marriage nearly every day—I want to keep him! We find we must date and flirt and do little things to deepen our love and commitment on a regular basis.

How does this apply to your customers? We get leads and do all we can to convert the leads to customers. We court them by offering specials, giving promotional gifts, putting on our best show. Once the customers purchase from us, we feel like they are "ours" to keep forever. Wrong!! No one "owns" a customer! Once you have won a customer, do all you can to keep that relationship healthy and strong. The courting part should never end!!

Lemon Aid Links: Service

MY OWN DEED IDEAS:

D

Dialing for Dollars

Anytime you pick up your phone—for both outbound and inbound calls—you're adding to your business cash register. When you think of your phone this way, you'll be more excited to initiate calls as well as answer them! I know some salespeople who calculate how much profit is generated from a phone call when a customer makes a purchase. Then they tape dollar bills (usually fake ones) representing that amount to their phone. Perhaps each time a customer orders from you your average profit is $50. Tape a real (or fake) $50 to your phone. This visual helps to motivate you to pick up the phone and dial.

Setting a goal for numbers of calls made every day or week will bring more dollars to you. This system really works. One year I decided I wanted to really create an increase in my sales. I calculated that I needed to call 40 people every week and ask if they were interested in doing business with me. Does that number overwhelm you? Break it down; in a week, it is just eight people per day. Make a game out of this challenge—and keep track of your progress and results. Choose the number you want to call and then Focus and Finish. By the end of the year that I just mentioned, I increased my personal sales $12,000 over the previous year.

Who do you call? All the leads you've met and then some!!
What do you say? Refer to the links in both Lemon Aid books.

Lemon Aid Links: Follow Through, Focus and Finish
Lead Alphabet: Telephone Books

Dialogue vs. Monologue

If you find you are doing all the talking during a sales presentation—a monologue, your sales will not be as good as if you involve the lead and ask for questions and feedback—a dialogue.

By doing all the talking, you miss pertinent information about the lead, and a dangerous thing happens. You assume you know what the needs/wants of the customer are.

Do all you can to involve your lead and/or audience. Find out what they like to talk about. Let them do a lot of talking and asking. Above all…LISTEN!

Lemon Aid Links: AAA: Attract, Ask, and Act

Do It—NOW!!

Another well-known secret to success. When making phone calls to leads and customers, I could talk myself in to and then out of making the call in the same ten seconds. I even came up with reasons why the lead would tell me "no." And, I knew calling at that minute wouldn't be a good idea because she might be fixing dinner, changing a diaper, or taking a nap. After getting really good at putting my business off, I found this secret. Do it and Do it Now! If the timing is not right, the lead will tell you. But you'll never know if you don't do it!

Whenever you find yourself putting off a task (in other words Procrastinating!), do a *TWIST!* Change the way you look at your task, hurry and do the task so you can cross it off your "to do" list. After a while, you'll look forward to things you used to hate to do! This is the technique I used to make myself do phone calling; now it's the favorite part of my business—because I did the *TWIST!*

Lemon Aid Links: Follow Through, Hot Potato, Quick

Drawings

Offer a drawing—at least monthly if not more often--for everyone you talk to about your business. This is another incentive for leads to give you their NAPEF. When you meet someone who appears to be interested in your product, ask if she/he would like to enter your drawing. I suggest saying, "Give you your name and phone so I can call you when you're the winner." They usually chuckle at your optimism.

Submit names for the drawing more than once depending on what sales action the lead/customer took: a purchase, a referral, attended a demonstration, and so forth.

You might choose to do the drawing at a monthly event to encourage excitement and attendance. Notify the winner, of course, but also call all the people whose names were in the drawing to offer "second place" or "runner up" gifts such as a dollar or percent discount off your product and thank them and schedule future business.

Lemon Aid Links: Educational and Entertaining Events, Profit Box

Lead Book: Purse/Pocket Presentations

MY OWN DEED IDEAS:

E

E-mail

Who doesn't use e-mail today? This has become nearly as common as using the telephone. Electronic communications can be an efficient way of keeping in touch with customers. E-mail could stand for Easy Mail because using this method is so simple; however, be aware of a couple of drawbacks.

When you take orders, **ask** customers for their e-mail address as well as their phone, address, and fax numbers (NAPEF). Emphasize the importance of printing clearly (one wrong letter and it won't work!). When I left spaces on order forms for e-mail information, I wasn't leaving enough room; some addresses are very long. Give customers plenty of room to write their electronic addresses.

E-mail notices of special promotions and sales as well as other pertinent information about your product/service/opportunity. One consultant said that she has an on-line newsletter that she sends out quarterly.

E-mail saves you time when your message isn't time-sensitive (use the phone only in that case). Do you have some customers who love to chat when you call, so you avoid calling because you don't want to get tied up? E-mail the message. I like e-mail when I'm working late at night. I can send a message without waking my customer up!

Sending e-mail greeting cards is fun for both the sender and recipient. You can send greetings for occasions you've never heard of. Try these sites: bluemountain.com, excite.com, Hallmark.com. These are just a few of many.

The drawback of using electronic mail is many people go for days without checking messages. Therefore, for dated information, a phone call is best; even if you have to leave a voice mail. Most people check these messages daily.

Another dilemma when using e-mail is sometimes the message doesn't go through and is lost in cyberspace. Or, if it is transmitted correctly, your customers sometimes have so many messages that yours could be overlooked. Keep this information in mind when deciding how to communicate with your customers.

Just as you want your customers' e-mail address, **give them yours.** Print this on all your literature. Check your e-mail box often and always respond; it's as easy as hitting the reply key!

Have your own e-mail address and box with an easy-to-remember name. If you share an address with your spouse or child, they may accidentally delete an important message. With all the free e-mail services, it is simple to set up your own, personalized accounts for no fee. Some web pages are hotmail.com, mailexcite.com, and yahoo.com.

Create your signature line with your name, mail address, phone (if you want to get phone orders—toll free works best), company name and business slogan. This information helps customers contact you much faster and easier. Most e-mail accounts have a way of attaching this to all your electronic correspondence.

Lemon Aid Links: Communication - Good News

Educational and Entertaining Events

We live in an information age; we crave knowledge, and we want to be entertained at the same time. To inform your leads about your product, business, and industry, hold related educational and entertaining events.

To convert leads to long-term customers, offer "how to" classes. Do you sell furniture? Offer a class on room arranging, wallpaper, accessories, etc. Is your business focused on health? Have a workout session at a local gym exclusively for your leads and customers, or hire a trainer to come and speak at an event you sponsor. If you sell makeup, invite your customers to an event where you have an image consultant give tips on wardrobe planning. You are not *focused* on selling your products at these events; however, I suggest a special offer for those in attendance only. If you have extra inventory, or out-of-date items, give some special prices. This is mainly a time to give your leads an introduction into what incentives you offer and to give your customers an added benefit of working with you while you educate them in a fun way on aspects of your business. Allow your customer to bring one or two friends (limit the number to keep the exclusive feeling of the event)—do a special drawing for guests only so you can capture their NAPEF.

I was a consultant to a start-up company who provided information on grocery shopping via the Internet on a subscription basis. Once a month, we had an educational event for subscribers and their guests. At these events, we had a speaker representing grocery stores, food manufactures, meat cutters, etc. Our goal was to enhance the information they were paying for through their subscriptions by providing additional resources.

These events can help educate customers on their new purchases. My brother recently bought a new car. Soon after the purchase, he was invited to the car dealership for an educational event. A buffet lunch was provided, and then the head of the service department gave useful tips about the car (how many of us really read the owner's manual?), and was also available for questions and answers. My brother invited my dad to go with him because my dad was interested in the same type of car. Both men were impressed with this meeting, and my dad ended up purchasing a similar car.

Send out invitations to these events (can be made on your computer), not flyers. This gives the feeling that customers are personally invited, not just announced. Require advance reservations so you'll know how many to plan for.

MY OWN DEED IDEAS:

F

Fax

Incoming faxes. Fax machines are becoming very common in both businesses and homes. If you don't have one in your office, invest in one soon. People can fax orders directly to you; they don't have to wait to get you on the phone. When you leave the message on your business line, tell callers that you offer a 24-hour fax service for their convenience at_____. Turn the fax machine ringer off so when you are on other lines, in meetings, or sleeping (if your office is in your home) the ringing won't interrupt you.

Invest in a dedicated line for your fax machine. You'll create a more professional image and also allow more business to be transacted via the fax. Your machine now becomes **another cash register**; but you have to let people know you provide this service. List your fax number on all your literature.

Outgoing faxes. Many of your customers have fax machines at their homes and/or offices. You can obtain customers' fax numbers when asking for their other information (NAPEF). Instead of asking "Do you have a fax machine?," ask "Do you have *access* to a fax machine?" Everyone has *access* to a fax machine. Copy centers, grocery stores, and even convenience stores allow faxes to be received or sent for a small fee.

When you have a special offer (this should be often), create a flyer with the offer and include an order form. Fax this to customers (remember you need to ask for the fax number!). If this goes to an office, you can be sure others will see the offer. Many faxes have cover sheets that alert all who see the fax that the following information is confidential and should be read by addressee only. Do a *TWIST* on your cover sheet, tell EVERYONE to read and respond. Be sure your customer's name is on the cover sheet so the flyer is not mistaken for junk. When you get a business fax number from a customer, let him know you offer this service so you have his approval to receive faxes at work.

When you **receive** faxes from companies and individuals, their fax number should be printed at the top. Put that number in a Fax Directory and **send them your offers**.

Lemon Aid Links: Communication - Good News
Lead Alphabet: Flyers, Reverse selling

Files

Have you been to a doctor's office and noticed the shelves and shelves of files? Why do doctors keep this information on their patients? So they'll have a record of each patient's illnesses and treatments.

Do your leads have illnesses you should be keeping track of? Of course they do. As a salesperson, your real job is helping your leads find solutions to situations they are aware of and unaware of. Your product or service is the medication they use to get well--until they become sick again.

Because you have so many "patients," doesn't it make sense to keep track of each one?

You have probably seen many different software programs on contact management that might work for you. However, I prefer a hardcopy, good old-fashioned file folder. This way, I can put correspondence/information that I receive *from* customers as well as what I send out to them. I also keep copies of their orders.

Why keep files on your customers?

1. You know what their previous problems were and what you did to solve them. This is much better than trying to guess and not come up with the previously-proven results. Or, if the solution didn't work, you'll know what *not* to do.

2. You have a record of what each customer ordered from you. If they can't remember or didn't keep information on the exact color, style, etc., you will be able to provide this additional service by opening your file.

3. Files add future profits. When you have a new product/service that is complimentary to what a customer already has or has requested, he/she now has an additional reason to do more business with you—if you inform them of the new product/service.

4. If a customer has need of the original order form to take care of service on the product and cannot find his/her copy, you will have this information at your fingertips; thus providing a valuable service.

Keeping good records also gives you a very professional reputation, and your customers will know they are important to you.

Focus—and Finish

When you have leads, sometimes you might get a little discouraged when you don't see positive results right away. This is when you keep your eye on your goal (converting leads to customers) and keep working.

Perhaps you gathered many leads at a fair exhibit. As you've been calling back on the leads (following through), you hear a lot of "I'm not interested," "Call me later," and maybe "Don't call me back again!" This is one of the rungs on the ladder of success you have to climb. Don't go back to the bottom of the ladder, or worse, throw the ladder down, which can be a tendency when immediate results are not made. Focus on the rest of the leads, and keep working until you've gone through them all.

Conversely, you might have some very positive results and decide that you've now "arrived" and don't need to call the rest of the people back. This is a big mistake. Keep focused and follow through. You're just tasting success—your goal is to feast on it!

One of my good friends was really excited about the door-to-door concept she read about in my Lead Alphabet book. She lived in a neighborhood of nearly 200 people. The first time she went out to "meet her neighbors," she got very positive response after talking to just 12 people. She excitedly called me with her progress. I was thrilled for her, but…reminded her that she still had over 190 more prospects in her own backyard who were waiting to meet her.

Perhaps you've set a goal to spend an hour a day in calling your leads. After 25 minutes you haven't talked to anyone but some answering machines! Keep going for the next 35 minutes. You never know when you'll strike gold; keep digging, keep focused, and finish!!

Lemon Aid Links: Follow Through, Telephone Tips

Follow Through

Look closely at the word, **"Follow".** Its meaning is "to come or go after; move behind and *in the same direction*." If you can only choose one deed to do out of this whole book, this is the most important. **Following through is the most important tool in building a business!!** And, here's a big secret. *This is the one activity people confess they do not do!*

I've known excited sales people who feel like they've "closed the deal" when all they've done is secured someone's name and phone and created interest in the product/service.

So, let's do the TWIST…notice the **double l** in follow. When I look at them, I am reminded of a ladder without rungs. In fact the ls could stand for "lead ladder." In converting a lead to a customer, you are simply guiding someone to where they need/want to go. Sometimes the lead is ahead of you, and you follow. Other times the lead is not sure, and your responsibility is to find what his/her wants/needs are and show them the rungs on the ladder that will lead them to that goal.

Rungs are not on the ladder yet because some people jump right to the top as soon as you present what you have to offer. These people only have two or three rungs to climb; others need rungs every few inches.

What are the rungs of the ladder or, How do you follow through? The answer depends on where the prospect is and what you've promised. Did you tell them you would **call, visit, or mail something?** If so, telling them is a promise. And, a promise made is a debt unpaid. Pay your debt to your prospect and do what you promised—immediately!! This debt of following through is how you bring profits into your business.

If you promised to send literature, samples, or other information, do so immediately, and then you must **follow through on the mailing.** The follow through is finished only when you've actually talked to the decision maker and learned how to serve his needs. If you mail a catalog, call a couple of days later to see that it was received. If the person tells you that he hasn't had time to look at it, ask when the best time would be to call back. Then ACT!! Call them back If you call, but the timing isn't good to chat, ASK when a better time would be, then ACT and call back.

I am amazed at salespeople who *pay* for advertising either by mail, fax, newspaper, or some other media and don't return calls or follow through on inquiries. Many times when I've called the number and left a message, I've *never* received a return call. I'm a hot potato, waiting to do business, and no response. These salespeople are literally running themselves out of business and paying money to do it!!
If you met the lead in a line at the store and struck up a conversation, she usually has more rungs to climb than someone you met at a presentation who is already familiar with your product. The person at the grocery store might request some

literature from you. Hopefully, you have it with you and can give it to her right then. She just climbed another rung. Is she at the top? If she looks at your literature, places an order and gives you a check, the answer is yes. If she says she'll go home and look over the information, she is still on the ladder. Ask her when she would like you to check back with her. I prefer to *ask rather than tell* because you are now letting the lead guide you as to what will be best for her. And, when you call, you are simply fulfilling her request. Timing is perhaps the critical element in following through. The best time to follow through is immediately. Or, when they customer has requested.

When she asks you to call her in three days, do it!! Remember, she has *invited* you to follow through. When you call her, she might say she hasn't had a chance to look over the information. While a variety of items can come to play here, you might ask again when a good time would be to check back, or maybe ask if now would be an opportunity for you to do a "phone presentation." This would be great if she was very interested in a particular product and now you both have a chance to talk specifically about it. Before you hang up, give her a *reason to take action* before you call back. Mention something like, "the products on pages 14 through 17 are on sale for half off until the end of the week. You can place your order over the phone with a credit card."

She has asked you to call back tomorrow; you do. She still has not taken any action. Now, you must find out if she really wants to be on your lead ladder or not. Ask, "Would you prefer to *call me* when you're ready to order/join the company/schedule a presentation?" This is a graceful way for you to let her off your ladder for right now. Some people say yes, others say, "Oh no, I really do need _____."

You must decide if you are willing to keep calling her right now or if she should go in your business bank for future contacts. I've found you can get a gut feeling for her interest and know if she really is interested or just stringing you along. My unwritten rule was to do three attempts. As long as I felt the interest was there,

I kept her name current. If, on the other hand, I felt like she enjoyed my calls because she got very few, and I am simply a social outlet for her (she needs to join my team!),I suggested she phone me when she is ready to do business. Then, I put her name in my business bank for the next month or two. I never discard a NAPEF! Sometimes the present time is not the perfect time for action. Keeping people on your ladder is fine if they still have an interest. My reply often was, "I will be happy to call you back as long as we both agree that I am not bothering you!" My customers knew I respected their time and in return they respected mine.

Many people who attend my seminars tell me of the time and money they spend in sending out packets of information and then complain when they receive no return calls or orders. These items will not ask for action—that's your role. The responsibility of follow through lies with the salesperson, not the potential customer. **A non-reply does not mean a no sale.** Remember, you will stand out as a true professional when you follow through. **You're never through if you follow through!!**
Options to repeat callings are to put the lead on a mailing list for new products, sales, important information. Or, invite her to attend an event. Most people need to be exposed to a product/service/opportunity five to nine times before taking action. Position yourself as a valuable tool so when someone receives communication from you, they will recognize you and appreciate your efforts.

So, here's an awesome idea. Set yourself apart from everyone else by being the absolute best follow through person known!! This is *easy to do, which makes it easy not to do as well.*

Lemon Aid Links: Do It, Hot potato, Quick

Frequent Buyer

Reward customers who are loyal to you. A frequent buyer program is one way to do this. If your company does not have a program in place, create your own within the guidelines of your company and/or promotional budget.

This program can be based on a dollar amount spent in a given time period or on units purchased. Examples: For every $250 purchased in six months, you'll receive a gift certificate for _____." You can give a gift certificate for a specified dollar amount or percentage off, or give a specific item as the bonus. Make the reward **achievable and attainable** so your customers will receive their reward, give you more residual business and profits, and also tell others about you.

If you have a highly-consumable product, I suggest a frequent buyer award based on units purchased. "For every five _____ purchased you'll receive _____ free." One of my friends, who sells candles, has a punch card that she gives to her customers. It is her business card, and for every candle purchased, she marks with a certain color of marker that is coded (so the customer cannot code it herself) or with a special punch that is available at craft stores. This is a guaranteed way to have your customers keep your business cards. Additionally, I suggest keeping your own record of the frequent buyers. **When you are working for a contest gift or sales goal, these are the first customers to call for reorders.**
Lemon Aid Links: Gifts with Purchase

Fun

You can have a lot of fun in your business. This doesn't mean you have to be a funny clown (unless that is the positioning you want). You can remain professional and have fun at the same time. Having fun is really nothing more than loving what you do and letting that love come through in all your actions. When you have fun, you become a magnet, and customers are attracted to you and your product, service, or opportunity and want to do business with you on a continual basis, or be part of your sales team.

MY OWN DEED IDEAS:

G

Getting to Know You

Once your lead does business with you, convert her to a lifetime customer by getting to know more about her, her family, and interests. I like to use a tool called "Getting to Know You." I have the following topics printed on 5 x 7 cards and have the customer fill in her information. So you'll understand the reasons for requesting each piece of information, next to each item, I've listed ways you and she will benefit when you get to know her. Adapt, add, or subtract topics to fit your business.

Name, Address, Phone, e-mail, fax (NAPEF): Most likely you have this information on an order form or in your data base. What if by some unfortunate chance the order forms are misplaced or you have a problem with your computer system? I love to collect recipes and have lost some of my favorites through the years. To prevent this, I write these favorites in more than one place. The same rule applies for NAPEFs. Have this critical, business-building data in more than one place. Ask for e-mail address and fax numbers. You will read ideas for using them elsewhere in this book.

Birthday: You'll want this date so you can send or e-mail greetings along with an optional gift certificate for your product/services. Refer to the ideas listed under "Birthdays" in this book.

Employer: Know the profession/company of your customer. If you want to do business with people in a particular company or industry, knowing specific people is very beneficial.

I believe you should do business with people who do business with you. If you are ever in need of your customer's expertise, you will add profits to her business by using her product/service.

If you meet someone who could benefit from your customer's service/business, you can be an excellent reference for her. Your customer will appreciate the referral and reciprocate by sending more customers to you, resulting in residual business and profits!

This information can also assists in recruiting. When you hear her company or industry has had a massive layoff, she might be ready to join your team or give you referrals.

Spouse's name: When you call or visit a customer, you will be able to personally call the spouse by name. Some of my best referrals came from the spouses of my customers because I got to know them. If your customer is not married, you'll know this without having to ask. Sometimes, the word "spouse" will be crossed out and replaced with "boyfriend/girlfriend," and his/her name will be listed. This saves you embarrassment by understanding relationships.

Anniversary: Because you now know the spouse and have started to develop a business relationship with him/her, you'll feel very comfortable in calling him/her before their anniversary and offering your product/service as a desirable gift. Make this call in time to have the gift ordered and delivered. Offer free gift wrapping. Even if a gift is not ordered, send or e-mail best wishes for their anniversary.

Children's names and birthdays: If you sell a product or service targeted to children, this will be very important information. I suggest beginning a Birthday Club for the kids. See "Birthday Club" section in this book.

Clubs, Organizations, Hobbies: What kinds of people do your customers hang out with? What does your customer do in her spare time? You will learn a lot about her interests and hobbies. If you find she has none, perhaps she'd like to join your team as a hobby. Or, maybe one of the organizations she belongs to is a prime target for a fund raiser.

Favorites: Knowing your customer's favorite food, restaurant, color, magazine, dessert, candy, movie, and holiday (just to mention a few) are helps in tailoring your product around her needs, and also gives you ideas of how to thank her for doing business with you.

If her favorite food is Chinese, and you have a new product that will help her prepare this food, call her. If your product line has added an item in her favorite color, call her. Simply do a TWIST on the way you look at her favorites and how you can show appreciation or offer additional service.

Products: Favorites and Wishes. The most important line of this card is to know what her favorite products are from your company and what she still wants. As the product line expands, items are discontinued, on sale, etc., you can call and target these benefits to her needs.

Lemon Aid Links: Anniversaries, Birthday, Birthday Clubs, Celebrations, E-mail, Fax, Wish Catalog

Gift Store

Gift store. If you don't have a retail location, consider setting aside a few shelves or an area of your home for a gift store. If possible, have these as cash and carry items. When you are talking to someone who is in need of a gift, invite them to come over.

My next-door neighbor, LaWaine Mohler, is a consultant for Jafra. She has a display of products set up in her dining room. Whenever I go over, I get to see what the newest products are, and I know she is an immediate source for gifts. If you don't have room in your home, set aside a gift box with gift-giving items inside. Have a few items decorated and some in gift baskets. Taking your gift box to demonstrations is a wonderful advertisement for announcing your gift store as well as showing your products as gifts and adding extra sales.

Or, create a virtual gift store by recommending gift ideas to your customers whenever they order from you. **Advertise your virtual gift store to your customers.** People might not perceive your product/service as a gift-giving idea. When you take orders from customers, thank them for their order and ask if they have any gift-giving occasions approaching. Just this simple suggestion will jog their memories, and you'll be amazed at the extra sales that you'll add. People are very appreciative of your reminder. Your customers are not always in the gift-giving frame of mind when they are buying products for themselves.

In my house, I have a "gift closet." When I am shopping and see items on sale, or something that reminds me of a particular person, I'll buy it and put it in my gift closet. This way I am prepared for those occasions that creep up on me. Suggest the idea of a gift closet or even a gift box to your leads. They will appreciate the tip and purchase your products even more often.

When gift seasons are nearing (Valentine's Day, Mother's and Father's Days, graduations, weddings, etc.), send or fax flyers to your customers announcing your "Gift Store" service. Incorporate these suggestions in your newsletter.

You can also do a TWIST on this and call leads to advertise your gift store and *then invite them to shop and order for themselves.*

The Booster (1-800-5JENNYB) has some great stickers and other tools for reminding customers about upcoming gift giving occasions.

Gifts of Appreciation. One of my friends, Stephanie, sells PartyLite Candles. She signed up as a subscriber with a grocery-information company I once consulted with. Because she was so grateful for the service I gave and the information she received, she gave me a lovely, huge candle that will burn forever, it seems. She really has me sold on her candles now that I have experienced them—all because she showed her appreciation by using her products as a gift. She taught me another way of expanding my business. Read on.

Contact spouses of customers to buy gifts. For Valentine's Day, Stephanie called spouses of her customers (including my husband—that's how I found out about this great idea!). She told them what candle their wife wanted. She offered to order, wrap, and deliver the candle for Valentine's. This really impressed the men.

To me, this was real customer service. In general, I've found that men put off purchasing gifts, and often don't get what their wives really want. Stephanie came up with a winning solution for all parties involved!

You can use the same approach for any gift-giving occasion. Use the Getting to Know You Cards to find out important dates in your customers' lives.

Lemon Aid Links: Calendars, Getting to Know You, Newsletters

Gift with purchase

I love to give gifts to show appreciation to my customers. If I have extra inventory of a product being phased out, I'll use it as a gift with purchase of a larger-priced item. Or, if my customer buys a large dollar amount at one given time, I am happy to give her a bonus! This little touch will help retain loyal and residual customers as well as their telling others about you.

The gift does not have to be expensive or extravagant; just very valuable to the receiver.

Lemon Aid Links: Frequent Buyers

Gift Certificates

Issuing Gift Certificates to customers who purchase large amounts of your product is a nice gesture and encourages future purchases. I advertised to my customers that for every $100 they bought, I would give them a five dollar gift certificate redeemable on the next order. This one hundred dollars did not have to be purchased at one time, but I specified a time period of six months to a year. This really works!! And, everyone spends much more than five dollars when they place their next order! If you have higher sales per customer adjust the figures to fit your business and profit structure.

Gift Certificates for apology. None of us is perfect, and I have certainly made mistakes on orders or in communicating with my customers! When this happens, I like to give an "Ooops Certificate." This is simply my apology for a mistake or an offense that I made. Relationships have been mended, and goodwill restored through this simple gesture.

Recording Gift Certificates. In a file or a binder, list all gift certificates that have been purchased by customers or issued by you. Note the issuing and redemption dates. This is a good system to remind people of their gift certificates and encourage their redemption. If you are working on a week or month of Super Sales, or are close to a goal, call people who are holding gift certificates from you. Typically, they will purchase more than the face value of the gift certificate. The sales will really add up!

Lemon Aid Links: Frequent buyer

MY OWN DEED IDEAS:

H

Holidays

As any holiday—Memorial Day, Veteran's Day, Easter—approaches notice how merchants capitalize on the occasion by offering sales and promotions to attract customers to visit their stores. Put your own TWIST on those ideas to focus on your customers' needs and how the celebration can *benefit them.* People get caught up in celebrations; especially when they benefit from the festivities. Sometimes the holiday can be your excuse for finally calling a customer! That is worth celebrating!

Focus your presentations on commemorating upcoming holidays. Plan these demonstrations a month or so in advance so the customers will have time to use the ideas and information you share and the products they purchase.

Be festive by decorating your literature and catalogs with holiday stamps and stickers. Use holiday-related, inexpensive trinkets as give aways. You'll find ideas for these at dollar stores.

Celebrate "proclaimed" days, weeks, and months like "Turn off the TV Day," "Ride your Bike to Work Week," "Take your Daughters to Work Day," "Earth Day," and so forth. Read national and local magazines and newspapers to find out about these days. Other salespeople probably don't notice these days, but you are unique!

You can even create your own holidays to honor your customers. If you have a popular product, proclaim, "Popular Product Day" (use the name of the item). Invite everyone who has purchased that item from you to join in the festivities!

Be sensitive to religious holidays as not everyone celebrates in the same way. And, be mindful of a holiday your customers might be celebrating that you don't observe. You can offer gift ideas and even celebrate their holidays with them!

Lemon Links: Lead Alphabet Book: Easter, Halloween, Honorary Days, Labor Day, Independence Day

Hot Potato

Now that you have leads--a name, phone, and address (NAPEF), you must act like this lead is a HOT POTATO! Don't hold on to it too long, or you'll get burned! This is how leads are. When they are hot, you must take action. The first action is to **contact the lead.**

The best time to contact a lead is as soon as you have initially met and/or they have expressed a desire for what you offer. They have you and your product or plan fresh on their mind. I've found many times that even if you call within 24 hours of your initial contact, their desire/want has waned a bit.

If your company is set up where a lead calls into an office and then the office contacts you, **call the lead as soon as you get the message!!** Perhaps the message is that the lead only needs service on your product. If you **assume** the person is not going to buy anything, and you put the message on the bottom of your "to call" list, you're making a huge mistake. First of all, most people will buy more product when you follow through on the service end. And, if you don't call back quickly, the lead will call someone else, or call your office and request another service person.

After you've made connection, you'll get a feel for how warm or hot the lead is. Is he ready to purchase right now? If so, give him simple instructions on buying the product NOW! Don't say "I'll call later to get your order." Be prepared to take the order, and the simpler the ordering process the more sales you'll make. "I can take your order right now; I accept credit cards, which one will you use?"

Is the person still undecided? Ask, "What haven't I explained about our product that you still need to know to make a decision?" Attempt to have the customer take action.

Does the person want you to call him back? Ask when and deposit the information in your Business Bank. Does the lead have friends who need your product and service? Ask for these referrals and get the names and phone numbers.

In preparing this book for publication, I sought print bids from a variety of printers. I made my decision and called my choice. I requested a more detailed bid, and told the sales rep I was just about ready to go to press. I never received a return call! I will not do business with that company. Consumers know that most salespeople give the best service before the sale, while working to win your business (I know you want to give great service all the time). When the pre-sales service is poor, it is often a prelude to what will happen as the relationship progresses. Unless the service person takes definite action steps to restore good will and confidence, the business is lost before it is won. And just as word-of-mouth has a positive effect, bad news passes even more quickly.

Take action immediately on **all** leads—you never know how hot they are until you make contact! Read on for ideas in determining the temperature and interest level of a lead.

Lemon Aid Links: Business Bank, Interest Assessment, Prepared to do Business, Service, User Friendly

MY OWN DEED IDEAS:

I

Interest Assessment

Perhaps one of the most frustrating parts of being a salesperson is trying to guess if your customer wants what you have to offer. So, don't guess—just ask, then act. The question, "are you interested?" is trite and not effective. First of all, it can be answered by a yes or no. Most people will say no even if they mean yes because we are conditioned to say no! A No is not always a No! So, we're back to the guessing game.

First, I suggest you not use the question, "Are you interested?" Rather, use questions that will help you get to know the person and what he/she really is interested in. Here are some examples:

"Why did you agree to meet with/talk with me today about my product/opportunity?"
The reason "why" we do something is usually our motivating force for taking action. When you find the reason why a prospect wants more information, you'll find out what motivates him/her.

"What is the best thing you heard about the product/opportunity?"
You'll find what is most important and interesting to the prospect with this question.

"If I could wave a magic wand and create the perfect product/opportunity, what would you want me to create?"
Maybe the product/opportunity you're describing or showing isn't at all what the customer wants, but when he describes what would be perfect to him, you might find a different product in your line more suitable.

"Using a scale of 1-10; 10 being the level of most interest, what is your interest level?"

In most cases, if the reply is five or under, this is the prospect's way of telling you now is not a good time to do business. However, when I've used this approach, and said, "Why don't you contact me when you feel you are ready to make a decision?", the prospect will say, "Oh, I am ready, what do I have to do to buy/get started?"

"What one thing would prevent you from purchasing/joining/signing up?"

People have to think about the "one thing" and many times will tell you more than one. This is another great way to discover why the are or are not choosing your product/opportunity.

"Are you serious about purchasing/joining or just joking?"

This is a pretty direct question (don't be too serious or joking when asking, just use a matter-of-fact tone). Because there are only two choices, you'll find a lot of information in this one-word answer.

"I don't want to waste your time or mine, is this something that will work for you/you want to buy/you want to try?"

This Yes or No answer tells the prospect you'll save him time by his answering the question.

"I am willing to put you on my call back list as long as we both agree that you're not being bothered."

This is an assessment statement for those prospects who aren't ready to do business right now, but are future possibilities. You're positioning yourself to call them in the future with their permission. The best thing is to *ask* when they want to be contacted. This way, you're calling them back with their *permission at their invitation.*

Using these questions and statement helps you assess if the conversation/relationship is worth pursuing at this time or in the future. For the futures whose names will go in your Business Bank or Alphabetical File, check back with them at the requested time, or when you are low on leads and long on calling time.

Keep in mind that you'll do 80% of your business with just 20% of your leads, and just because the answer might not be positive right now, future follow through could bring some very profitable results…even juicy profits.

Internet

The Internet is a terrific tool for building a business in many ways. I love the Internet for communicating with my leads and customers. Of course, you can use e-mail and a web page. Here's another idea. Create a list for your customers to subscribe to at no cost. While many sites exist for setting up your list, I have been happy with onelist.com. Go to that web site and you can register. Join my list, onelist.com/subscribe/lemonaidlady.

How can having a list help you grow your business? First of all, you will have a target audience of people who want your information. They have to register to subscribe. Put you list along with your NAPEF on all your literature and when you do presentations. Position this as a valuable service you provide at no cost.

The list is helpful because not only can you use it for communication, but your subscribers can submit ideas, information, and requests of their own, so everybody learns! I prefer to have a moderated list which means I read all e-mails that subscribers submit. I decide if this information is worthwhile for the entire list, which adds value to the no-fee subscription. You can even create a list where you are the only one who can send out messages.

Use the list to give ideas for using your products. Other subscribers will submit their own ideas and experiences which will entice more subscribers to order. You will learn valuable information from your customers.

Unless you restrict your list, anyone, anywhere can subscribe. You can share your information with people all over the globe.

From time to time, I have special offers just for my list subscribers. I announce these offers just a few days before I send the offer. This way, I can encourage my subscribers to contact their friends and anyone who would be interested in my product to hurry and subscribe. My special offers run for just one or two days.

Have you joined the lemonaidlady list? Log on now!

MY OWN DEED IDEAS:

J

Juicy Profits

The goal for all businesses is to make a profit. Hopefully we all have a passion for our product/opportunity/profession. Even so, if we did not receive some type of reward, we would not be as inclined to pursue new business.

Here's a choice for you. If I were to give you a shiny, bright, juicy lemon or a wilted, shrunken, hard, dried-out lemon, which would you choose? If you want to quench your thirst, you'd certainly choose the first lemon. Do you realize both lemons took about the same time to develop from a seed into a full-grown fruit? The difference was the juicy lemon is at its prime. It is ready to have the juice squeezed. The dried-out lemon sat too long. It wilted and has little juice to give. Many of the ideas you'll read about in this book deal with prompt follow through; contacting leads when they are in the prime stage of deciding to do business with you.

You are the one responsible for squeezing the juicy profits out of your business. While you're squeezing, would you rather yield a lot of juice or just a little? The entire focus of this book is to teach you ways to get more profits out of the business through referrals, relationships, retaining your customers, and reaping residual profits.

Even with a juicy lemon, there are still ways to yield more juice. If you like culinary tips, try pressing your hand on top of a lemon and then rolling it on a counter top before cutting it open. Or, heat the lemon in a microwave oven for about 30 seconds before cutting it open.

The way you yield juicier profits is to hold your prospects tightly to you (squeezing) and then warm them. Building relationships will help you retain residual customers and in turn bring sweet successes and juicy profits.

K
Kids

One of the benefits of having your own business is to be able to work around a family's schedule. If you have children, or interface with customers who do, here are some deeds that will add profits to your bottom line.

Customers' Kids. A great measuring stick of how good you are at retaining customers is when you begin to service a second generation of customers—your customers' kids. After twenty years in selling, I have begun to have the privilege of servicing this next generation. Kids grow up fast. When you service the in a pleasing manner, kids notice and will want to work with you as they have needs of your service or product.

Because I marketed my product primarily though group presentations in people's homes, I got to know my customer's kids. This is a great opportunity to get to know the family— many times I felt like I was part of my customers' families! Learn the children's names and something about them. One of my favorite kids is Kiersten McIntire. I knew that she loved pink. So each time I went to her mom's home, I took her something pink, even if it was just pink bubble gum! When the kids look forward to having you visit with the parents, they are usually better behaved.

Which brings us to the next issue. How do you handle kids who are misbehaving at presentations or in a retail location? Have something specific with which to entertain them; this makes them feel special as well. When I did presentations, I often took a box of toys that the kids could play with. I did this so they wouldn't disturb my display. This tactic didn't always work, but it sure helped! Moms appreciated that I considered their children. When I had a business where my customers came to me, and often brought their children, I had a tent full of plastic balls where the kids could play. This kept them contained in one place, and they weren't running all over the office. If you do provide this extra touch, keep in mind the issue of liability (too bad that we need to consider this), and have insurance coverage if needed.

If you sell child-related products, having items set aside exclusively to entertain the kids is one of the surest ways of boosting your sales! Kids really are great persuaders, and if they want something, mom and dad are very inclined to make the purchase if they see the kids using and enjoying the product.

Have surprises to give to the kids. When kids came into our place of business, my husband always had little trinkets to give to them. They loved coming to visit Bob! Have a container with prizes or treats to award the kids for good behavior while they are in your place of business. As a caution, be sure the prize is not too small to be swallowed. Balloons are not a good idea, and be cautious about giving out candy—ask mom's permission first. I personally like stickers. They are inexpensive, kids love them, and so do moms.

Your kids. If you are a parent, perhaps one of your motivating reasons in starting your own business was so you could spend time with your children. This is one of the reasons I am an advocate of having your own business—you are more in control of your time and family.

Next to not wanting to be a pushy salesperson, the next excuse I hear for not performing, usually revolves around kids. Many people use their children as an excuse for not working rather than the reason for excelling in their profession.

As a mother of three sons, two of whom were not born before I began my own business, I am very aware of the challenges of combining family and business responsibilities. While entire books are written on this subject, let me share a couple of tips to help you so you'll have more customers buying more products, so you'll have more profits.

Involve your kids in what you're doing *to the extent they want to be involved.* When my boys were younger, they loved to help stamp catalogs. I let them practice on old catalogs first, and then they could advance to doing the real thing. My desire was that they would want to get more involved the older they got. They didn't. We owned a franchise operation, and my boys had many opportunities to work in the business, but the two younger weren't very interested. However, our oldest son in high school did work in our office.. And although we had some conflicts at work (which is typical in a relationship with a teenager) he was able to develop his organizational skills and helped us a great deal in establishing office procedures, filing systems, etc. Today he thanks us for what he learned about business while observing us for many, many years.

While it is good to involve your children, be choosy about what involvement they have. Match the task to their ability. As cute as it may seem, don't let children answer your business phone. If your kids do help stamp or sticker your literature, be sure this is done properly. An older elementary-age child could be assigned to be box products, carry display items to your car, unload your car, or wash your car. Kids as young as junior high are computer wizards. Entering customer information into a data base is a great job for a qualified kid and frees you up from that monotonous responsibility. The bottom line is, kids who see their parents manage successful businesses, have some responsibilities to assist, and then reap the benefits, are more prepared to enter the market place when they are old enough. What a valuable gift you can give your children! A gift money cannot buy.

What household jobs can you hire your kids to do? When my son was in sixth grade, I asked him what he would charge me to do the laundry twice a week. He gave me a bid of $5 per week. At the time, it was a lot of money for him, and not having to do laundry freed me up. My boys now cook for me, do laundry, clean bathrooms, and other homemaking chores.

Your business will come first—sometimes. My lifetime priority is family before business. However, there are times when business does come first. One Saturday morning I was holding a team meeting. Afterward, one of the consultants came up and said she had to quit her business because she needed to spend more time with her kids. The interesting thing was, she had hardly done anything! She was simply on a guilt trip. I explained that she would feel less guilty if she planned time slots for working, and let her family know that during those few hours, business would take precedence. Then, when she was away from the business, she wouldn't be feeling guilty that she wasn't working. Children need to learn that you love them even if you cannot give them your attention-on-demand. Just as the Bible tells us there is a time for every season, there is a purpose for every hour. Plan and fill your work time both as a business person and as a parent accordingly.

Knowledge

A lead will add dollars to your pocket when you are in the know about:

Your customer: If nothing else, know and remember your customer's name and something else about her—this tidbit of information also helps you remember her name! After that, any other information you know and remember about a customer will be impressive to them. We all like to be known for who we are. When you take the time to acknowledge your customers and something unique about each one, they will *remember you* and your thoughtfulness and want to be a life-long customer.

Your product: Many people say "my product sells itself." If this were true, we'd all be without opportunities—the products could all be sold via mail order or on the Internet! (I know both of these modes are viable, profitable ways of selling; however, more sales will come when you first establish relationships along with offering these services.) Your product knowledge sells the product along with its reputation and word-of-mouth endorsements. If customers have a choice between an order taker and a service person who cares about relationships, knows the merchandise and gives informative use and care tips, the latter person would be chosen.

Become passionate and knowledgeable about your product. I've heard people say, "I'll sell the product, but I can't afford to buy it." What kind of message is coming across? You'll be a better salesperson and service person when you become your own best customer. How can you persuade someone to purchase your product or service when you aren't even convinced?

Your industry: Do you sell candles, kitchenware, Internet service, vitamins?? Whatever your industry is, keep abreast of new developments.

Recently I was shopping for a new health care insurance policy. The agents I talked to educated me on some new terms dealing with dental insurance. However, one agent said, "I've been in business over 30 years and have never heard of that; it's not important for you to know either." Sometimes we get cemented in old habits. This doesn't work in today's market place. You have to be familiar with the trends of your respective industry if you're going to persuade customers to do long-term business with you. Read publications covering your business and attend as many educational functions you can.

Your competition: When you are aware of the information your customers find when they "shop around," you'll be a better resource and salesperson to your customers. You will know how to position yourself to appeal to your customers' needs and set yourself favorably apart from the competition.

Lemon Aid Links: Competition

Kindness

The opposite of kindness is rudeness. Have you ever been serviced (that's a contradiction in terms!) by someone who was really rude? Some people believe *they* are doing *you* a favor by servicing you. Actually, each party is dependent on the other and should act as such. The salesperson would not sell anything without a customer; the customer wouldn't have a service person without the salesperson. Always be kind to both customers and people who service you—even when the kindness might not be returned.

When you are contacting leads, remember you might be the only bright spot in that person's life that day. Smile (even if you're talking over the phone) and be very pleasant. If the prospect is not interested in your product/service, he will remember you as a kind person. Next time you call (of course I know you'll keep in touch, if only for referrals), he will be receptive to your call. This has often led to business that otherwise would not have been transacted or referrals that might not have been given.

One of my first jobs was at a retail store selling fabric. I used to service some very unhappy people. When I complained about this type of customer, my mother taught me to "kill 'em with kindness." Lest you think this is something violent, what you are killing is the meanness and rudeness of a person when you treat them with kindness.

After one of several cross-country moves, I was becoming irritated with the culture of my new area. My business was not growing. I was not producing nearly what I had been in my previous area. I was frustrated and depressed. And, I was taking this out on the customers and hostesses I did have. I was not my usual, helpful self. One day while driving to an appointment, a thought came to me, "It doesn't matter how much money you make, it matters how you treat people." That thought, years later, continues to stick in my mind. I started being more kind and stopped focusing on me and focused on how I could help my customers and hostesses. I became a more kind person, and my business GREW!!

Even though this is a book of ideas, it is an appropriate place to share an inspirational poem:

Regrets
You may be sorry that you spoke,
Sorry you stayed or went,
Sorry you won or lost,
Sorry so much was spent.
But as you go through life you'll find—
You're never sorry you were kind.

L

Lists

Lists are helpful tools in following through with customers' requests for products, updated catalogs, birthdays, and call backs. Don't trust your memory to think you'll recall who wants what and when you're to call people back. While you can use a contact management system on your computer, a piece of paper (full-size; not scrap pieces) with a title, names, and phone numbers work well. This simple organization will help you expand your business base because you'll have a systemized way of servicing your customers.

TWIST on lists: To achieve your goal in helping people feel appreciated and special, thus adding residual customers to your business, identify your lists with **unique names.**

Maybe List: If a customer is undecided about purchasing or committing to a presentation, suggest putting her name on the "Maybe list." This is a gentle approach; very non-threatening. She'll recognize that you'll be calling her back at her request. (Remember the concept of asking, "When do *you want* me to call you?") Caution: don't put definite "yeses" on this list—they are already committed and just need to be contacted at a future date. These people should go on the "gift list."

Celebration List: Put customers' birthdays, anniversaries, and other recognition occasions on this list.

Profit List: If you have a business opportunity and the prospect is not ready to join right now, tell him you'll add his name to your Profit List of people who prefer profits—rather than "I'll put you on my call back list." Everyone else has a "call back" list. Yours is unique! When you do a *TWIST* on the list name, he is reminded that you and your opportunity will lead him to profits.

Gift List: Usually we make up a gift list for things *we want*. The *TWIST* on this is to put names of people you want to *give gifts to*—hostesses or those who give you referrals.

While you tell your lead about the "special list" you're adding her name to, I still consolidate all names in to my Business Bank for easier tracking and contacting. You can note which list the name came from to refresh your memory as to the approach you take in the follow through.

Lemon Aid Links: Business Bank, Internet

Literature

Your published sales materials are a direct reflection on you. This literature is often the key to new sales as customers have a something tangible to remember you with. All information should be neat, clean, and appear unused (I recycle and reuse when the materials have been gently used). Your name, phone, fax, and e-mail should be listed on everything you hand out. I believe your customers should always have current literature from you, and that you should pass this out freely. Literature includes newsletters, brochures, business cards, promotional offers/flyers, and catalogs.

Catalogs: One of my customers was complaining about the price of the company's catalogs. Her friend had a great reply, "Try selling the product without them!"

Catalogs can be costly if you don't use them correctly. Otherwise, they are a real advertising bargain.

Positioning the Catalog for Value. When you give someone your company's catalog, briefly explain the features of owning this literature.

Many companies have catalogs that include information other than just products for sale. Items such as recipes, hints, educational information, use and care instructions for the product, and more are often contained in a product catalog. Instruct your customers to keep their catalog in a safe place; perhaps with other instruction booklets, with cookbooks, by the computer, and so on. Depending on the product you sell is where you would suggest the catalog be kept. In other words, encourage them to keep the catalog in a place where they will remember you.

When I give a catalog to a customer, I position it with a *TWIST*. I explain, "This is a **Best Seller!** (isn't your company's catalog full of best selling items?") I would love to give you a complimentary copy to keep if you would like it. You must promise me that you'll store it in a safe place so every month when you order from me, you'll know where to locate your catalog." (Notice how this emphasizes reordering.) "However, if you don't want to keep this best seller, please return it to me. I'll only be offended if you take it and throw it away."

Free or Fee? If you don't have to charge your customers for catalogs, give them freely—but show the value of the catalog before handing it out using the idea above.

If the size of your catalog is such that you must charge customers for it, position it differently than "you have to pay for the catalog." Instead, offer this as a **subscription** to your product and services. Most of these larger catalogs are valid for six to 12 months. Suggest they "subscribe" to your catalog and service for just $_____ (catalog price). Because they are now a "subscriber" offer free subscription extensions when a certain dollar amount is spent within a specified period of time. For example, "When you purchase $150 or more in the next six months, you'll receive a new catalog at no charge because you are a subscriber." (Choose an appropriate purchase amount for your company.) The subscriber concept is almost like joining an elite club—give these customers premiere attention and service. These are the first people to contact when working on a big week or month of sales. They already have a catalog and a relationship with you.

Pass the catalog on. Customers often ask if they can have a catalog for a friend or family member. I was happy to give them information to promote me and my business. Go a step beyond just giving catalogs away, and ask the customer for the names/phone numbers of who they are going to give the catalog to so you can call to service them. If the referral orders, give the referring customer a referral reward. Remember, referral rewards don't have to be expensive, only perceived as valuable. Thank you notes are terrific!

Outdated Catalogs: As long as the new catalog doesn't have a huge price increase and the majority of the items are still available, I use the older catalogs to hand out to people I meet away from presentations or store location to create interest. Many times, I'll put these on the windshields of the two cars on either side of me in parking lots. If the person is interested in an item that is no longer available, I explain that the offer just expired. Most of the time, people want the "tried and true" regular line items and I never had a problem with this.

Some of my co-workers who had huge inventories of close-dated literature contacted their local papers. For a fee (cost depends on many variables), the newspaper will insert the catalogs in the paper. A potential "throw away" could result in many customers and profits!

Lemon Aid Links: Wish Catalogs

Lead Alphabet: Grocery Stores—parking lots

M

Mailings

On a regular basis, send out catalog/product information to those who like to be kept updated on your product. Target those who are frequent buyers, catalog subscribers, and preferred customers. You can also add to this list by asking people if they want to be updated on your products. You can divide these customers up into thirds or fourths. Once a month, do a mailing to one group. This way, everyone hears from you three to four times a year, and you're not overextending your printing/mailing budget. More importantly, you have better opportunity to do follow through phone calls to several smaller groups rather than one large group. as If, after five or six mailings, you get no response in way of orders or requests for service, take the name off of the mailing list, but don't discard the NAPEF.

If you are going to mail the identical piece out to at least 200 people on a regular basis, check with your local post office about doing bulk mailing. Remember, bulk mail will take longer for delivery, so don't send time-sensitive materials unless you allow sufficient leeway.

For the best response from your mailing investment, **follow through with a phone call** to be sure the information was received and to ask for new business and/or referrals. The response rate for direct mailing is very low; usually one percent. However, you have a targeted audience who know you. This, coupled with a follow up phone call will dramatically raise the percentages.

Don't expect a piece of literature to do the selling for you—it just prepares your customers for a call from you to personally invite them to do business. The exception to not having to do follow-up calls is when you have an exceptional direct response ad where the customer is so enthralled with your offer, he picks up the phone and calls YOU! Do a lot of test marketing to find ads and offers that will accomplish these results. Until then, follow through.

Some salespeople have the mistaken idea that the bigger and more expensive the mailing package the better the response. This is not true. A seminar attendee told me she put an ad in a newspaper and spent over $2500 sending packets out to the people who called on the ad. This consultant was upset because after all this, she had no positive results! She was depending on the literature in the mailings to convince the leads to call her; she made no follow through phone calls. This was a real waste of $2500!

Magazine Articles

Read magazines and find stories and articles that are appropriate for inclusion in your personal or group presentations. If these are "how to" tips, try them out first before sharing the ideas.

You might find articles that remind you of a specific customer. Send the article to the person with a note. The customer is so impressed that you not only remembered her, but also remembered something about her and want to help her learn more about her business/hobby/life. The same concept works with other printed media like newspapers, newsletters, etc.

Magnets

Do you want your customers to "stick to you"? Use magnets. I've already told you how to make a magnet out of your business card. You can make your own magnets out of anything you want your customers to keep when you use magnet sheets. To save time, however, I suggest ordering the Booster catalog (1-800-5-JENNYB). Jenny sells terrific magnets at very, very, reasonable prices. I use these constantly. Just today, I received a postcard from a customer-turned-good-friend. She said that she thinks of me every time she sees my magnet on her fridge.

If you sell a "big ticket" item—cars, furniture, computers, appliances, a magnet with your NAPEF is an effective gift to include in the thank you note. Having magnets reminds you to write the thank you notes because you need something to send along with the magnet. Don't just hand the magnets out; add value by mailing them along with your thank you.

When a customer scheduled a demonstration with me, I sent her a magnet with the demonstration date and time written on it as well as my name and phone number. Where did my customers put these magnets? On their fridge, of course. After the demonstration was delivered, I sent her another magnet with a thank you message along with my name and phone number. Every time this customer, who is now a hostess, had a demonstration, she received at least two magnets. Could she ever forget that I was her service person?

The far-reaching effect of this is when friends and family of my hostess visit and go to the fridge, they see my name, company, and phone number. Now, these new leads call me, and my customer base is multiplied!! Such a simple, inexpensive, personal touch with great residual results.

Lemon Aid Links: Appreciation to customers, Business Card Magnets

Merchandise

The condition of the products you have for display, demonstration, and distribution says volumes about you as a salesperson. Be sure that everything is clean, blemish-free and unused!!

Some companies do cooking or craft classes where the items need to be used at the demonstration. Using a new product each time would not be practical. Some clothing companies have the guests try on clothes at the demonstration. Obviously, the clothes will have been tried on by people at previous demonstrations. These are exceptions to the above suggestion. However, these items should always be clean and neat. If something begins looking "shop worn", sell it at a discount and purchase another new item. The continual rotation of your merchandise keeps things looking sharp and impressive.

Whether you deliver your product in person, at a demonstration, or a few weeks later, treat all items with TLC. Check for any scratches, discoloration, or even torn packaging. When your customers get their merchandise, they expect brand new products. Sometimes, the bags holding the products will be ripped. Use new packaging. All these little attention-to-details make a world of difference in converting leads into long-term customers and residual profits.

Lemon Aid Links: Appearance

Message Books

Purchase spiral bound message books with duplicate copies from your local office supply and always keep one by every phone. This way, you'll sound much more professional when taking messages. Customers won't hear you say "wait a minute; I have to find something to write on." And, when you go to refer to the message, you won't be looking for little scraps of paper! This is really beneficial when you're retrieving messages from your voice mail. Everything is in one place.

So, how does this help you convert leads to customers? Many times people will call you with a simple business question. They might not be prepared to purchase anything or to join your team, but they are important. Because you didn't actually transact any business, you won't have a record of the conversation anywhere but in the message book. Save these books. A couple of times a year, go through them and call some of these people. You'll be amazed what results you'll achieve!

I even record the e-mail messages in my book and note that I have responded to a customer's request. This record is a wonderful tool in following through; especially if you did not receive a reply to your e-mail response.

Lemon Aid Links: Telephone Tips

Miracle on 34th Street

Remember this classic Christmas movie with the *real* Kris Kringle? He is the Santa at Macy's Department Store, but sends people to the competition when he realizes that Macy's is out of a popular item. The customers are so impressed, an entire advertising campaign is formed from this concept. and Macy's sales soar. Santa was the supreme service person by acting in the customer's best interest, rather than being concerned solely about the sales/profits at Macy's. Yes, that was a fictional story. However, I know from experience that when you work in the best interest of the customer, their trust level grows, and they will do continual business with you.

When a lead calls you, and you know your product/service is not the real solution to her problem, know where you can refer her to. The next time your name or product name is mentioned, she will tell others about you as well as purchase other items from you in the future.

Lemon Aid Links: Competition, Knowledge

Mobile Customers

Because we are a mobile society, many of your customers will be transferred out of your area. Let them know you can still be their consultant. Get their new address, and mail them new catalogs. A nice touch is to send a gift basket with your products to them as they move to their new home. This would be a great recruiting idea because your customer will let her new friends and neighbors know about you and your service. She/he would likely want to join your team to service all those referrals in her new area. A bonus with this approach is she gets to keep in contact with you.

If your business is not conducive to long-distance distribution, do a *TWIST*. Obtain the customer's new NAPEF. With her permission, forward it to someone else in your company or industry in her new area. Establish relationships with other salespeople in other cities so you can share referrals. If desired, decide on compensation program.

Before your customer leaves town, ask her for any other referrals in your city. I've attained some of my best customers this way.

Multiples

When a customer buys something, ask if she needs more than just one. Offer suggestions for multiple uses for that item. Or, remind her of gift giving occasions. She might add more than one of that item to her order. She'll thank you for the additional suggestions even if she doesn't need more than one because she now has multiple uses for the item she purchased, which adds value to the product.

MY OWN DEED IDEAS:

N

Newsletters

One of the best ways to educate and inform your customers about your product and service is to produce a simple newsletter. This is not a sale flyer, even though you will want to mention any specials. The main purpose is to educate, inform, and entertain so they will want to purchase your product and continue to be a loyal customer. Above all, focus on the customers—not on you. A colleague recently wrote that the first couple issues of his company newsletter went over okay, but not great. When he targeted the news *to be about his customers*, the response and excitement rate rose.

You can recognize a current customer by doing a feature story about how your product helped this person.

Highlight a consultant on your team or an employee and show how the product/business opportunity helped her.

Ask for contributions from your customers. If they have tips or suggestions, include those. People love seeing their name in print! Do a "Dear Abby" column where customers can state their problem, and you will give a solution using your product line.

Subscriptions. Free or Fee? This depends on the publication. Can you produce this yourself with a computer program (Microsoft Publisher has a nice template), or do you have to pay for the services of a graphic artist? Do you send to under 200, or are you sending to thousands? There are too many variables for me to make a suggestion. Whichever way you go, **show them the value of their subscription.**

Add gift certificates and offers just for these subscribers.

Lemon Aid Links: Mailings, Preferred Customers

Newspaper Clippings

If you've read *The Lemon Aid Lead Alphabet*, you know that one of my favorite ways of getting new leads is through the local newspaper. Once you have these leads and get to know more about the people and their interests, you can use the newspaper to communicate with and recognize them which helps to add residual customers and profits to your business.

Subscribe to the local papers in the geographical areas you do business in and read them. Watch particularly for news about people, not just events. Are any of your customers/leads in the news? Have they been promoted in their company? Have they participated in community and civic events? Did you see an article about one of their children (refer to the "Getting to Know you Cards to know the names and ages of their kids)? Cut these articles out and mail them to your customer along with a congratulatory note. They will really be impressed that you noticed their accomplishment and that you took the time to send a copy and a note.

Using the "Get to Know you Card" will also help you learn about their interests. When you come across an article in a newspaper or a magazine that relates to her interests, clip it and mail it along with a note that you were thinking about her. These two ideas will add sales indirectly to your business because you are building relationships for long-term business!

Lemon Aid Links: Celebrations, Getting to Know you, Magazines

Neighbor Drop By

Have you ever had someone drop by to visit just because they were in your neighborhood? In most cases, you were probably delighted to have the unexpected, spontaneous company. If you weren't thrilled to see them because you were interrupted or ready to leave, at least you were cordial and invited them to come back, right? (Remember what goes around comes around; always be nice to everyone.) Use this idea to help expand your business.

Many times I've had business in an area and either finished early or someone postponed at the last minute (a nice way of saying I was stood up!). This is a great time to do the *TWIST*. You can either be upset, or twist the way you look at a situation and go visit someone else.

You can simply drop by, or perhaps call from your car while parked near your customer's home or office. When you say that you are out in front, people laugh and invite you to come in. Many times I have far better results with this spontaneous visit than with the visit I had planned.

If this doesn't work, and you still have time for face-to-face visits, do the "on both sides" approach. Go to the houses/apartments/offices on both sides of your original or spontaneous appointment. Tell the occupants that you know _____ who lives next to them (you have your foot in the door because now this is not a cold call), and wanted to service all the neighbors. The amazing thing is most people know their co-workers better than their neighbors. So, you've made a connection with the new person and helped her get to know who lives next to her. If you sell your product through a demonstration plan, you have someone to add to a guest list!

Lemon Aid Links: Profit Box

Lemon Aid Lead Alphabet - Door-to-Door

Night Before Calls

The night before your scheduled one-on-one, face-to-face appointments, call to confirm the meeting with your lead. Some of my friends didn't like to do this because they thought the lead would have an opportunity to cancel the meeting. Guess what?

If a lead is not interested, she'll cancel anyway. Why waste your time? Your phone call shows that you are a professional and that you run your business on a schedule which shows you value your time and hers. Other professionals remind customers of appointments (doctors, dentists, hairdressers, etc.) so should you.

Notes

We all love to get hand-written mail on colored stationery— mostly because bills aren't sent this way!! Be observant and watch for reasons to send or leave your leads and customers notes.

If you were in their neighborhood, and they were not home, leave a nice note. If you are recognizing them for an achievement, write a note. Maybe you saw/heard/read something that reminded you of them and wrote a quick "thinking of you" note. Any type of communication keeps in contact with your special customers which retains them as *your customers* and brings residual profits to you.

Here's a *TWIST* on sending notes. When you are generous with your praise, praise comes back to you. You will begin to receive notes and thanks from customers! I keep all my notes in a "love basket." This is a little pink, plastic, heart-shaped basket in my office. Some days when I need a little boost, I'll read one of these love notes from my customers. I've even used comments from these notes as testimonials.

And, because we are all human, you might get some complaint notes as well as compliments. Use these as suggestions to improve on your service and performance. Keep these filed away, and if you ever need a piece of "humble pie," read these.

Lemon Aid Links: Appreciation, Magazines, Newspaper Clippings, four Rs

0

Objections

After you have a lead's NAPEF, and you attempt to convert him to a customer, you'll most likely get objections as to why he cannot or will not do business with you. I love objections and LISTEN to them. Unlike some sales training I learned early in my career, I **do not try to overcome objections**. When I focus on "overcoming objections" I feel like I'm not really listening to the prospect, but instead, thinking ahead of the conversation as to how I can counteract the objections with my own ideas and opinions.

Instead, listen with empathy and with a matchmaker mentality. By listening, learn where the person is mentally and physically with his situation After they have "bled" out all the details, simply talk with them about possible solutions. Sometimes you'll have answers; sometimes you won't.

My philosophy is **"meet someone where they are before you take them to where you want/they want to go."** To do this, you need to know "where the prospect is"—not in a geographical sense, but in relation to what you are offering/what he needs or wants.

However, this concept can be illustrated with a geographical example. If I am in Nome, Alaska, and I want you to join me, I need to **know where you are** so I can give you directions and guidance. Are you in Norman, Oklahoma, or Northville, Michigan? The routes for traveling to Nome are different from both locations—just like each lead is at a different location relative to what you have to offer.

Next, I can talk all I want to give you directions to Nome, but what if you have no desire to go to Nome?? Or, even if you have the desire, would you rather have me go with you or just tell you what to do. I believe this works for leading customers to do business with us. We **listen first and then lead**. Sometimes you'll send a lead to Alabama instead of Alaska. Do what is in the best interest of the prospect; he'll respect your listening and honesty. Read on to learn about **seeing** a lead's needs...

Lemon Aid Links: Miracle on 34th Street

Observation

One of the most critical ways in converting a prospect to a customer is by *observing what they do and listening to what they say*. This is perhaps the way you found the lead in the first place. I believe everyone is "bleeding" in some way. Watch and listen for their "bleeds" which are their "needs."

If you sell clothing, your lead might mention she is really busy right now because she is returning to school and must buy a new wardrobe. In the same sentence she "bleeds" by telling you she knows little about fashion and has a budget as big as her fashion knowledge. (I did not make up this scenario.) Rather, I read it recently in a woman's magazine where a lady wrote a letter to the editor. This woman was bleeding and advertising it to the world!! If you are observant, you'll be able to stop her bleeding and show her solutions. Thus converting her to a customer. Sometimes leads don't know their needs, and you can help with this discovery.

Lemon Aid Links: AAA: Attract, Ask, and Act

Overbooking

Give the appearance that you are in demand, and people will flock to you. Have you ever noticed we all want what we can't have? Companies with a very slow-moving product will end production. Now that consumers can't have it, they want it!

The same works with you as a professional sales person. If you tell people you can meet with them "whenever you want," they will normally not take quick (or any) action. However, if you tell them you have limited appointment slots and offer one, or maybe two choices, they'll jump at the chance to meet with you. You have now positioned yourself as a busy, knowledge professional who is in demand. People want to work with the best; allow them that opportunity.

One morning my son complained of an earache—a frequent occurrence. We were new to the area, and I called a doctor from my insurance list. The receptionist said I could come in any time that day! That worried me. I wondered, "If the doctor isn't busy, how can he be any good?" So we drove to his office. Without even stopping my car, I could tell by the looks of his building and parking lot that this was not the kind of ear doctor I wanted my son to see.

If I am looking for a new hairstylist and am told I can come in anytime, I know she/he can't be too good of a stylist, or she/he would be in demand, hard to get in to and many times overbooked!

Until you are actually overbooked, you can create the appearance of being so. Block out times in your calendar when you do want to service customers. Fill the other time slots appropriately with other activities. When someone wants an appointment with you, say, I have _____ or _____. I believe in offering two choices if I have two slots available. If neither of those work, offer one more. Most people will take one of those three choices. If someone has too many choices, they take forever in making a decision, or they don't make a decision at all. The worst thing you can say is "business is so bad, I can meet with you any time." You've just lost a customer.

Lemon Aid Links: Waiting List

MY OWN DEED IDEAS:

P

Packaging and Perception

My college-age son was complaining during his first semester at school that some of the girls attracted to him weren't the kind of girls he wanted to hang out with. He is a really smart kid and astute business person, but he thought having a tatoo and a nose ring was a good idea. When he realized the type of crowd he was attracting, he changed his ways after I pointed out an important aspect of marketing—packaging.

Manufacturers spend millions of dollars creating appealing packages so we'll buy their products. We do judge books by the covers and products by the packaging.

What is your packaging? Who are you attracting? What perception do people have of you because of your packaging?

If you want to attract a certain type of clientele, look at your packaging. How do you dress, talk, service people, treat people, demonstrate your product, or anything that people *see* you do? This is all part of your packaging that creates a perception. And, perception is reality.

If you want to create or change the perception others have of you, position and promote yourself accordingly.

Lemon Aid Links: Positioning and Promoting

Persistent Professional or Pushy Pest

In sales, one of the excuses for non-performance I hear most often—and I do call this an excuse—is "I don't want to be pushy." No, you don't want to be pushy, but you do want to be persistent. Let's look at the differences.

To push is to "exert force and move away." Of course you wouldn't want to *force* a customer into taking action because they will *move away* from you, thus defeating everything discussed about relationships in this book.

Persistent has a motivating meaning: "to hold firmly and steadfastly to some purpose, state, or undertaking, despite obstacles, warnings, or setbacks; to be tenacious."

If you're being pushy, people will ignore you and not want to visit with you because you are more concerned about making money and selling your product than servicing their needs. On the other hand, if you have a strong belief in your purpose, if you are loyal to that belief, your product, and yourself in spite of difficulties or challenges, and your focus is on helping others, you are a persistent professional. Only jealous souls will call you pushy in the latter situation. Don't listen to them.

If people move away from you, you're being pushy. If they are attracted to you, you're being persistent. Don't be pushy, but don't be a pushover. Get to work; your responsibility is to tell about and sell your product/service/opportunity. Open your mouth and begin lifelong service and sales relationships.

Phone Presentations

When you have a hot lead and have a hard time connecting to meet, schedule a phone presentation about your product/service/opportunity. Mail or fax any materials needed for the presentation ahead of time, including order forms, opportunity agreements, or anything else needed to complete the transaction you are discussing. When you have someone who is ready to buy/get started, don't embarrass yourself by having to say, "I'll have to mail you the order form/agreement." Decide on a specific time for **you to make the call** (don't count on the lead to do this!). Have all your materials in front of you and call promptly at the designated time.

Go over the materials just as if you were in person. The biggest drawback is you can't observe body language. So, you must listen very carefully. Let the lead do a lot of the talking. And, at the end, ask for action. If you wait for the lead to volunteer, not much will happen. Some people call this closing the sale. I prefer to keep an open relationship with my customers, so I feel like this is really the beginning of a long-term relationship.

You might get the response that they need to "think about" what you have told them. Ask if you have left any questions unanswered so that while they are "thinking", they'll have all the information. Then, *ask* when a good time would be to call back. Hopefully, you won't have to do this last step because the lead will be so happy with you, your service, and your product/opportunity that they will not hesitate at all to take action.

Pictures of People using your Products

Whenever you have the opportunity to see customers using your products, take some pictures and create a scrapbook to show at demonstrations or posters to hang in your place of business.

Why would pictures help you convert leads to dollars? Everyone is different. You might attract a certain type of customer profile, but not all types. So, when your leads see someone who remind them of themselves, they can more easily picture themselves using your product or joining your organization.

You'll also learn ideas from your customers as you watch how they use your product. Why? Because now instead of walking by, you are literally, through the camera, focusing on what they are doing. You become more observant. Now you have new ideas to share and use, and the results are recorded on film.

Positioning and Promoting Yourself

What do you want to be known for? What do you want people to think of when they hear your name? You have the power to place yourself in your prospects' minds the way you want them to perceive you. But, you must have a plan and make it happen. If not, customers will come up with their own positioning and perceptions of you.

Do you want to be known as the "kitchen clown" because you sell kitchen products in a humorous and educational way? Or, would you rather create your position as a "personal home economics consultant?"

Be the **first** in your field, be the **best** in your field, or be **unique**. **Unique** is usually the choice, unless, of course, you are the first or the best. What about you will set you apart from others who might appear to be just like you—people in the same company or profession? Do you have a unique business card, literature, handouts? What icon do people associate with you? What kind of a *TWIST* do you put on the way you service your customers? How will you make your presentation unique so you'll be remembered? These are all questions you must ask as you position yourself for success.

Associate yourself with a memorable icon. After reading this book and/or attending my seminars, who will you think of when you see a lemon? The Lemon Aid Lady, Christie Northrup, of course!! (Sometimes you need to remind your audience that they will remember you when they see your icon, and then they do remember—power of suggestion.)

Once you have decided how you want to position yourself, promote yourself according to your positioning plan (no one else can do this in the beginning).

Create a slogan stating your purpose for being in business. Tell the world, print it on all your literature, announce it on your voice mail. As The Lemon Aid Lady, my purpose is to **"Teach you**

how to *TWIST* sour situations into Sweet Successes and Juicy Profits!"

Promote yourself as the expert in your field and in your customers' minds by learning all you can about your industry, product, company, and most of all about your customers. The ideas you read about in this book will help you in this promotion and positioning.

Lemon Aid Links: Packaging and Perception, Sell Yourself

Preferred Customers

Many companies have a program like this. I suggest doing a *TWIST*. First of all, come up with a unique name that coincides with your company, product, or purpose. For example, I call my "preferred customers"--people like you who buy, read, and listen to my Lemon Aid Products--**Lemon Aid Learners**. Something catchy is more appealing than "same old, same old."

Ask your leads if they'd like to be part of this group. I get mailings every day telling me I'm a preferred customer (a worn-out title). Funny thing, all my neighbors get the same mailing, so I don't feel very "preferred."

If a lead has to subscribe to be a member your preferred group, she will understand its value. You can have customers register by checking a box on an order form, filling out a registration card, or calling/e-mailing/faxing their request. When she gets information from you, she knows it was something she requested, not a mailing list she was dumped into.

As a business owner, I want my special offers to go out to those who are interested in doing business with me. Now, this doesn't mean I don't send things to other people, only that my **Lemon Aid Learners** are unique because they have *chosen* to be part o this group. It's a relationship we both want.

Notice I didn't say anything about being on a "preferred customer list." But the concept is the same. And, you are preferred because I don't send the complimentary newsletter to everyone who buys this book, only those who take the time to register with me. Thanks for being a Lemon Aid Learner!

Lemon Aid Links: Internet

Prepared to do Business

As a business owner, always be prepared to do business. Using the ideas from this book and the Lead Alphabet, you will meet leads everywhere you go. Be prepared to do business.

How? Carry sales catalogs, literature, business cards, order forms, applications and a pen and paper *with* you. If I sat by you at a sporting event and discovered you sell something I need, I'd be very impressed if you had *something* to give me to take action. Or at least, begin a sales dialogue.

Especially be prepared when you are going to appointments and doing sales presentations. I am very amazed at salespeople who ask for the order, get an affirmative response, but don't have order forms or other supplies necessary to complete the transaction.

If you do product presentations to groups, have new materials to give to new customers who schedule future presentations with you. If you don't have them immediately available, the customer's interest will fade and you'll possible lose out.

Profit Box

Just like your phone is a cash register, anything containing business records is another profit center. In this section, I'll share some ideas for physically keeping track of leads' names as well as a system you can use to convert the leads to customers.

My preference is a simple 5" x 7" file box with alphabetical and monthly tabs. Yes, I realize that we live in a computer age and many great contact management systems exist. I use those as well. However, I am much better at selling than I am at being a computer guru. And, I make more money at selling than at data entry. So, when I am working and have a hot lead, rather than spend time going to my computer, I write things down on a hard copy. In non-prime time (when my customers are sleeping!), I can take an opportunity to input the information, or better yet, hire someone to do this task.

Computers work well for the convenience of printing mailing labels and tracking customers in a data base, but I've seen many potentially great salespeople waste time learning new software, surfing the Internet, etc. Be careful how much time you spend with technology. **Keep focused on the profit part of your position**, not the non-profit.

In my Profit Box, I file my leads alphabetically as I get them. The lead cards can be the "Getting to Know You" cards (the lead has written the information so you don't have to), a business card taped on to a 5 x 7 card (this way the card doesn't become lost), a drawing card, or an index card I've created myself with a customer's NAPEF. When someone asks me to call back, I can move their card to a monthly tab. However, I find my Business Bank works best for this. Find one that works for you.

The monthly tab can also be used for filing the contact cards by birthday or anniversary. I suggest keeping the main card filed alphabetically. I believe that putting NAPEFs in more than one place is safe business practice. In case of tragedy, you'll have a backup system in place.

You can have more than one file box (you'll need it for the amount of customers you'll have). I suggest rather than stretching out the alphabet, that you file according to geographical areas. This way, if you have an appointment on the south part of your area, take the file box for that area. You never know if you'll be finished early or have someone "postpone" at the minute you arrive. Now, instead of wasting time, you can go see other customers. Or, if you have one appointment set up on the west side of your area, and remember a couple of other people you'd like to see while you're driving in that direction, you can go to the file with that geography. You don't have to waste time going through the names of all your customers.

As I talk to my leads, I write down notes of the conversation on the backs of the cards. If a lead moves, or information changes, staple a new card to the existing card. All this information can be transferred to your electronic data management system and/or put in your business bank.

Lemon Aid Links: Business Bank, Files, Getting to Know You, Neighbor Drop By

Profiles

What are the characteristics of your ideal customers? Where do they live? What are their ages, hobbies, professions and incomes? What is their family life like? Do they have children? How many?

When you know the profile of your ideal, targeted customer, you'll be able to find more people like them. You'll find the profile answers when you use the "Getting to Know You" cards.

You could pay big bucks and buy targeted mailing lists. My belief is find the customers and leads you already have who fit this profile. Then, ask those people for more and more referrals.

If your "perfect" customer is Wendy Patterson, look on her "Getting to Know You" card. Find out what her favorites are. Now, call Wendy and ask her for more referrals who are similar in profile to her.

Lemon Aid Links: Getting to Know You

Promises and Projections

In the excitement of securing a sale and new customers, I've heard a lot of sales professionals make unrealistic promises. The result is disappointed, upset, mad customers who take their business elsewhere. Everyone loses.

I learned the hard way (after promising the unrealistic) that giving projections are better than giving promises. Projections are anticipations. "I'd project that the delivery will be next Wednesday." People will out right ask, "Is that a promise?" I only promise if (1) I am completely in control of the situation and (2) the promise can be fulfilled immediately.

For example, I can promise you I'll hand you this pen I am holding. Or, I can promise you I'll drive you to the store right now. Beyond the present, I don't know if I'll be around to drive you to the store next week. I can project that I will be able to, however.

If I'm very confident of a projection, such as a delivery date, I take my projection out a couple days beyond. If I tell you that your order should be delivered on Thursday, my real projection is Tuesday. I believe a customer would rather be happy that you're early than mad that you're late, or that the item is a lower price than the projected higher estimate.

Lemon Aid Links: Communication

Q

Quality

A continual debate between quality and quantity exists. I believe you can and should have both. Quality should be in what you give to your customers. Quality of service, knowledge, and products. You might not have control over your company's products, but you have control over the quality of service you give people. *TWIST* your view of quality as something you *give*, not *get*, and you'll receive quality business and profits in quantity.

Quantity

Quantity comes in the number of people you talk to. The number of leads on you list. The amount of units you sell. The total of your profits. Quantity doesn't mean the amount of time you have to put into your business. All time should be quality time. So, quality and quantity are important but do not describe the same things.

In analyzing your progress, use the *quantity* as a measuring stick, not percentages. If you only have one customer, and gain another, you've had a one hundred percent increase! Sounds impressive, but is it really? Percentages have their place, but numbers, or quantity, are where the results really are.

Qualify

If you've purchased a home, you know that one of the first things a real estate agent will do is qualify you for the price range of a home you can afford. This process saves time, disappointment, and frustration. You can avoid these same feelings by qualifying your leads. Because you'll have a large quantity of leads, you need to see who is really qualified to purchase your product/join your organization and who isn't. This qualification can be done by asking pertinent and appropriate questions.

Is your lead the person who makes the decision in the home/organization about your product/opportunity? Does the lead have to financially qualify for the purchase? Is there an age requirement? (Minors are legally not liable for contracts; therefore many direct selling companies will not allow them to join.)

I've found many people who are most willing to do business with me are those who are least qualified. I've had young people with a desire to hold demonstrations; however, they are not the decision maker in their home (although they usually have a lot of influence!), and their mothers did not agree. A woman without a phone or a car was eager to join my team, but those are two absolute necessities (at least the phone) in having a business. Create a bridge for future opportunities with this type of lead, but don't waste your present efforts.

Lemon Aid Links: AAA: Ask, then Act, Interest Assessment

Quick

When you have a lead, take quick action to convert him/her to a customer. You don't want to hold on to it for long or you'll get burned. Believe me, I know. More than once, I had a very interested lead who I knew would do business with me. So, instead of contacting her immediately, I called other leads who I had to persuade. My thinking was the warm lead was a "for sure," and I could call them anytime.

I was very wrong. These leads were ready to do business NOW. When I didn't contact them immediately, they either phoned someone else in my company or industry, or someone else in my company or industry phoned them. I am a firm believer in the saying "when the student is ready the teacher appears." Well, here's a TWIST on that. "When the lead is ready, the salesperson appears, and if the salesperson doesn't follow through, another salesperson will." Be quick. Always call your warmest leads first. Otherwise they will get cold and you'll end up with leftovers if there are any of those left!! And, they never taste as good as when they were first hot!

If this idea sounds repetitious, it is. This is one area where every salesperson needs to get perfect at—following though in an urgent manner!

Lemon Aid Link: Hot Potato, Follow Through

MY OWN DEED IDEAS:

R

Referrals, relationship, retention, residual

I consider these the **four R's of growing a business**. To this point, you have leads, which are referrals, for your business. The ideas in this book will teach you how to develop relationships which translates to long-term customers resulting in residual profits. Study this section, memorize the concepts of the four R's, and you'll have an abundance of Sweet Successes and Juicy Profits!

Referrals

After you have found new customers, rely on and expect those valuable people to tell others about you, your product, and service. Of course, the key to this is to turn all your customers into "raving fans" so they'll tell all *their* friends and family about you.

Service will be discussed in the next section of this book. So, let's talk about how to get referrals. I believe that while you are presenting your product/opportunity to your leads, they are thinking to themselves, "I bet Angela would love this product." Or, "I can't wait to tell Elizabeth about what I bought." So, ASK for referrals, and then take ACTION.

After you assist customers with an orders--in person or on the phone--ask, "Who do you know that would also benefit from this product/service?" If you are selling in a demonstration setting, many people have already been thinking about who they would invite to their own demonstration, but they usually talk themselves out of setting a date with you. This is why *inviting* each person to give referrals or host a presentation is so critical; they have usually been considering this anyway!

When a customer gives you referrals; contact them soon. Often, customers request they contact the family/friend first to introduce you before your call. This is wonderful! In fact, I recommend suggesting this approach. You now have a warmer lead who has already been given a recommendation about you! Always thank the referring customer, and if business results, consider giving referral rewards.

Do a *TWIST* on the Frequent Buyer program, and create a **Repeating Referral Reward.** Reward your customers for giving you a certain amount of referrals in a designated time period. One way I've *TWISTED* this idea and expanded my business is asking people who were the most excited about my books to have at least ten other people call and order my book. This system is great because the leads are *calling you.* Just remember to ask (as you always should when you get a call from any new customer), **"Who can I thank for referring you to me?"** This shows the new customer that referrals are important to you. Then I gave the referring person a copy of the book as a reward. This helps everyone. More people heard about and benefited from the information in the Lemon Aid books, the referring person received a free book, and I met new customers I would not have otherwise known. If you love what you're reading and want to share the information with others and be rewarded, call my office at 940-498-0995.

Lemon Aid Lead Alphabet: Referrals

Requests

Do you listen to a radio station where listeners can call in requests? Have you ever called in and had a song played that *you requested?* You probably felt flattered that your request was chosen. I love those stations because so many people are giving input that a wide variety of songs are played—some I've never heard of but have enjoyed listening to.

Ask your customers for requests (this *TWIST* of a term sounds more fun than the typical "suggestion"). Listen to and implement as many requests as you can. Sometimes a combination of ideas will result in a real burst of business. Be very open to requests and ideas from the people who want and use your product. Realize some people will complain when they are really giving a request. You must listen—and learn. They really are experts because they have used your product/service. Thank the person for the request. If you implement it any form, let the customer know. Companies spend millions of dollars on consumer research to squeeze suggestions out of people. All you have to do is *ask for requests*. If one person has an idea, others— including you—will benefit from it.

As you meet new customers and leads, they might ask for variations in your product lines by giving you requests. Your company might or might not come up with what the person is requesting. Sometimes the request is simple such as a color change. Many times the customers have very elaborate ideas for new products. Regardless, let them know you take their requests very seriously. Tell them that you will put them on a special list and will get back to them when and if the item becomes available. Sometimes, companies will discontinue a product for a while. If the item comes back, you will drive yourself crazy trying to remember who wanted it. Sometimes the exact item will not be available, but something closely related will. In your schedule book, have a page to list these people. You can title the list requests, ideas, whatever will match your needs. Just be sure to put the persons NAPEF and pertinent information about what they want.

Lemon Aid Links: Lists, complaints

Return Phone Calls

In our high-tech world of voice mail, we never have to answer our phones or personally talk with anyone. We can play a continual game of "phone tag." However, I've seen the trend go to not playing the game at all. In other words, not returning any phone calls. We feel like we can choose who to and who not to talk to; which is our prerogative. However, you never know who the person really is who is calling. It could be your next recruit in the guise of someone needing some service on your product. You figure if you don't return the call, someone else will help her. And someone will. Returning phone calls also shows professional courtesy.

When I get a call from a salesperson who asks me to return his call, I try to do so right away. I like to keep goodwill within the selling industry, and I believe we can all learn from other sales people. If I am not interested in the offer, I honestly say so. This way, he doesn't have to keep trying to connect with me. Wouldn't it be nice if the leads you leave messages with would return your calls (even though you shouldn't *expect* them to because that follow through is your responsibility)? I believe what goes around comes around. Return all phone calls left on your voice mail and see if more people call you back when you leave messages.

Lemon Aid Links: Telephone Tips

MY OWN DEED IDEAS:

S

STP

If you are knowledgeable about cars and engines, you're probably thinking this is the name of a product you put in your engine to get better performance. You're half right. STP has everything to do with increasing performance, but nothing to do with cars or engines.

This is an important concept that I learned very early on in my sales career. In order to be an effective service person, you must **See The People—STP**. When people purchase your product/service or join your team, you are part of the reason they choose to do business with you. If someone doesn't like you, they'll probably decline any offer you give.

How can you increase the number of people who like you and like doing business with you? See The People!! When customers can see you and know you, they are more comfortable doing business with you and your company. Remember one of the four R's to creating residual profits is relationships. You establish relationships by knowing your customers; you know them by seeing them. Group presentations are a profitable way of seeing the people!

And, let the people see you!! Perhaps you have a business that is primarily done over the phone or Internet where you don't have a chance to personally see people. Give yourself a lot of exposure so potential customers feel like they know you because they see you.

Lemon Aid Links: Educational and Entertaining Events, Internet, Mailings, Newsletters

Schedule

If you are going to have a business, you must create time slots for business-building tasks. Even if you work your business on a part-time basis, you'll never grow until you schedule time to work.

My suggestion is to have a weekly, routine schedule that allows for flexibility. Plan blocks of time for doing the most important part of your business: marketing! Through the years, I met many potentially-successful people. They never made it because they spent time working on their computer, organizing the office, calling co-workers, going to lunch, putting together sales literature, and other "busy" jobs. None of these tasks are necessary if there are no customers. **Finding customers and following through on your leads is the most important responsibility you have in your business.**

Granted, doing the other above mentioned jobs are also a part of running a business. Spend early mornings or late nights (non-prime time) doing these. Prime time is when your customers are awake and waiting to hear from you. If you must perform these tasks during prime time, keep the allotted time as short as possible. As your business grows (or maybe you're already at this stage), hire other people to do what you can delegate. You'll pay for others' services, but then you can do what you do best: selling and servicing new and existing customers which will add huge profits to your bank account.

Sell...Till you Excel!

Here's a *TWIST* on the "Shop till you Drop" idea. Selling, like any other profession, has challenges. I believe it is one profession where people give up too easily. I've also observed those who practice the most perform the best. In other words, they **sell till they excel!** If you are nervous or frightened, that's okay. Being prepared by practicing reduces tension. In other words, **Performance, and Practice, relieves Pressure!!** When I was new to sales, I practiced on my one-year-old and his stuffed animals! Then, I actually used the "practice" method to sell. If I had a prospect who claimed no interest, I asked if I could simply "practice." I was at ease because I realized I really had nothing to lose—the person already told me he didn't want my product/opportunity! The irony was that often, my practice customer ended up being a real, lifelong customer after seeing what I had to offer.

Sell Yourself...to yourself... before you sell anything else!

Before you can be an effective salesperson for your product/service/opportunity, you must believe in what you are selling. But, before you can believe in what you're selling, you must believe in YOU!! When you realize that you are your own best asset and an important resource to many people and the means through which they can obtain a desirable product/service/opportunity, your sales will increase.

Customers want to do business with a person who is sure of him/herself. Confidence is not cockiness, but a surety that you are valuable. As your confidence increases, so does your customer base and your sales, and then you gain more confidence. This is a wonderful circle of growth—personally and professionally.

How do you gain this confidence and self-assurance? Here's an easy idea. Make an advertisement about you! Use some of your own photos along with pictures from magazines. Create an ad showing your strengths, interests, personality, and goals. Next to this write down all your good qualities. Every day add something positive about yourself to this advertisement collage. As you exude a confident air, you will begin getting complimentary notes. Keep these in a Love Basket and refer to them often.

Lemon Aid Links: Notes

Service

Books have been written, talks have been given, and examples have been illustrated about customer service. Yet, the level of customer service has still declined. Walk in many establishments and you sometimes have a difficult time finding someone to help you or answer your questions. If you do find a clerk, she is not always knowledgeable about the products she sells or cares about helping you. This is why relationship building is so critical to sales success.

Here is another area, like follow through, where you can really set yourself apart from your competition. Really care about your customers. Don't be concerned about the money you're making from a sales transaction. Focus first on the customer's needs and wants and be sure the transaction is fulfilling these needs and wants. Keep in mind, as you begin a business, you'll do a lot of activities that you won't get paid for. As your business grows, you'll get paid for a lot of activities you didn't have to do—in other words you'll create residual income from establishing a solid service base. A good friend, Pattie Chwalek, once counseled me, "Take your eyes off the dollars, and the dollars will fall in your wallet."

Read as much as you can about ways to improve the service you give your customers. This book contains many examples. And then practice, practice, practice. Become the best customer service person anyone knows. Learn from bad examples and good examples. Keep a journal of your successes. Remember:

Service

And

Love

Equals

Success!!

Lemon Aid Links: Requests

Set$

A lead will choose to do long-term business with you when you give exceptional service. One way is to show and sell your products in sets. You're probably saying, "How is showing my customers more products a way of servicing them?"

Because showing sets is not just showing more products. You are showing more uses for the products so that customers will get more value out of the product.

If you purchased a beautiful jacket and went home and realized you had nothing to wear with it, you'd be disappointed. The jacket would most likely hang in your closet until you felt like going shopping to find matching skirt, pants, and blouse. Hopefully, you would eventually find a match.

However, if the jacket would have been shown with all the coordinating pieces, you would have had the option of purchasing those pieces and now you could wear your new jacket.

When you show a set of complementing products, give the price for the set. People tend to want the bottom line—so just give the final price. Usually, they'll take the entire set, even if the price isn't discounted. This is because they don't have to take the time to add each thing up themselves. You create and price a package deal and customers buy it.

Lemon Aid Links: Complimentary Products

MY OWN DEED IDEAS:

T

Teach

In all my years of selling, I've considered myself more of a teacher than a salesperson. My first responsibility has been to educate people on a problem they were experiencing or a situation that could be avoided by using my product/service. A true salesperson educates the prospect on the product and industry, and an effective teacher cares about her students and their progress. The profits made on the transaction is really compensation for teaching; not for selling. **The more you learn, the more you earn; the more you teach the more you sell.**

If your company has an opportunity for recruiting, you'll talk to many people who say they are not a "salesperson." (They use the term as if it were the lowliest of professions, when in fact salespeople are among the highest paid!) Assure them you are not interested in a "salesperson," rather, you are looking for a teacher.

Telephone Tips

Since you're reading this book, you probably have your own business. Run your business like a business and install a separate business line—or at the very least a custom calling line, which is a separate phone number with a distinctive ring so you know when a customer is calling, and you can answer appropriately. If the phone is in your home office, don't allow your family members to answer this line unless you have instructed them in the proper business manner of answering your phone and taking messages. Never allow young children to answer the phone or record the message for your business. This is unprofessional and might turn some leads off before they even talk to you.

The telephone is the life line of your business!! It is your cash register! Verbal contact with customers will build relationships which help ensure their doing future business with you. Of course the telephone is not the only mode of communication, but I feel it is probably the most important one. You can mail information and hope it gets read. You can e-mail and not know when someone will retrieve it. You can fax messages and have an error in transmission without knowing. But the telephone is an audible instrument. People hear their phones ring or listen to messages left on voice mail or answering machines.

Leaving Messages. Remember common phone etiquette. The first recommendation is to **speak slowly.** I was using my mother's phone one day and left a message on someone's voice mail. She overheard me and asked if I thought the person who listened to the message would have been able to have understood it, especially my phone number, (a critical piece of information) because I spoke too quickly. Now, every time I leave a message, I remember my mom's statement, (aren't moms wonderful!) and I am reminded to talk slowly enough so the person can write down the information I am leaving.

Renee Cole, a director for The Pampered Chef, shared some insights with me about the way we say phone numbers when leaving messages. Our phone numbers are ten digits (this includes the area code which must be dialed in many metropolitan areas and always with toll calls). Renee reminded me of the natural rhythm to repeating a phone number. We usually say the first three, the next three, and then the last four. If you run these digits together in a different rhythm, people have a difficult time writing and remembering your phone number. This happens a lot with computer-generated messages. Keep this idea of rhythm in mind when telling people your credit card and social security numbers. Take a breathing break when you see a break in numbers. The listener will be better able to communicate with you, resulting in fewer mistakes.

I also believe in leaving detailed messages if doing so will speed up the service I give my customers. Perhaps an item or color number was not recorded on her order sheet. I give her the reason for the call, and when she calls me back, if I'm not available, she can give me the information so I can speed up her order.

If the message is solely to begin a relationship, I am brief and promise to call them back. I leave an enticing reason for them to return my call, if they wish. Sometimes the prospect is very interested in your offer and can't wait for your return call. Say "In case you're too excited to wait for my call, you can contact me at _____." Or, "For your reference my phone number is _____," This gives the prospect an option; not a command.

I've had sales people leave me messages "putting the ball in my court" to do business with them without showing the benefits of my returning the call! I am more offended when the return call costs me money to make. Likewise, many sales people complain to me that customers don't return their calls. This non-action on a prospect's part does not mean she doesn't want the product or service. She just doesn't have a reason to say yes—yet. Leave your name, number, and message so your prospect can return your call, as discussed above, but expect that you will be the one who should call back.

Answering the phone. Answer the phone on the third or fourth ring. If you're too busy to answer the phone, you're not in a position to talk to a customer; let the message go to your voice mail. Speaking slowly is especially important when answering the phone. If you run any type of business, even out of a home office, answer the phone in a professional manner and voice. Identify the company and/or yourself in a positive, uplifting voice. Have you ever called a business, had a person on the other end answer the phone, and you couldn't understand the name of the business? A customer who is calling a business shouldn't have to wonder if they have reached the right place.

When you identify yourself or business, speak slowly and clearly. Just this morning I called a business, when the owner answered the phone, he said his name and company so fast, I didn't know if I had reached the right business.

When you answer the phone, be thrilled your cash register is ringing!! Before you answer, pretend the person on the other end is calling to place the biggest order you've ever had. You'll be energetic and excited! No one wants to pursue a business relationship with someone who does not like what they are doing. I realize sometimes this takes a bit of acting. You might have just received some bad news about not getting a new account; maybe you're doing some tedious book work and are in a serious mode. Maybe you are involved with your family. When the phone rings, you must be an enthusiastic person. If you're not in a mood or situation to take a call, let it go to voice mail.

Lemon Aid Links: Return Phone Calls

Testimonials

The best sales people are your customers and clients. Word of mouth truly is a great form of advertising. You will get many letters, e-mails, calls, and notes thanking you for your product/service. Ask the giver for permission to use these quotes promotionally in marketing your products. As consumers, we tend to believe our peer group—other consumers—over the sales person or manufacturer.

Keep a file of all testimonials and create a scrapbook with these letters and comments. Add pictures of your customers using the products.

If you are not getting testimonials, ask for them. People love your product, they just haven't taken the time to write or verbalize their delight. I have one friend who gives his customers a form letter to begin the thought process of testimonials. They can fill in the blanks and add their own opinion. He then asks for the letter to be typed on the customer's own letterhead or stationery.

To obtain testimonials from participants at the Lemon Aid Seminars, I ask: "Who is the first person you're going to tell about this seminar when you leave?" (Now you also have a referral). And then, "What will you tell him about the seminar?" This becomes the testimonial.

Testimonials help when you have a certain type of customer who can't picture himself using your product. When you present a testimonial of a customer who fits the same profile, all of a sudden his perspective changes.

Lemon Aid Links: Notes, Pictures of People Using Products

Tracking

Part of leading leads to doing business with you is keeping track of the leads you have!! Believe me, I've written plenty of names on little pieces of paper and have lost them. My favorite place then became the check register of my checkbook!! This is a very poor system for something as important as your business. Treat NAPEFs as if they are money—they are!

You can simply keep a small notebook in your purse or pocket, or have a page in your calendar book—whichever item you have with you most often. Creating a purse/pocket presentation also is a great tool for this.

After you contact these potential customers, keep their information in your business bank, file, profit file, or computerized contact management system. Track how many customers you talk to before making a sale. Then set your goals. If you want to make ten sales in a week, and you usually have to talk to eight people before getting a sale, make your goal to talk to 40 people in a week, or eight each day! Keep record of your results activity and results. Some days, you might think you've talked to 32 people, when you've only talked to 12! Keeping track will keep you on track!

Lead Alphabet: Purse/Pocket Presentation

MY OWN DEED IDEAS:

U

User Friendly

In this high-tech, information-overloaded world, keeping customers means creating a user friendly atmosphere.

Remember that your customers don't work in your business every day like you do. Using your company/industry lingo confuses a prospect. Explain your business and products in simple terms.

The easier you make the ordering process, the more orders you will get. If a customer can dial your phone number (at no cost to her), give you her order and credit card and have you deliver or ship the product, you will have many orders. If the customer has to fill out a complicated order form, make a copy, find an envelope, write a check, buy a stamp, and then go to the post office, you won't do the same volume of sales.

One of my friends bought a number of large furniture items from her local furniture store. Picking out just the right colors/styles/patterns was quite the chore. However, she relates, when she went to have the order written up, the transaction became a nightmare. Although the store was completely computerized, the salesperson couldn't find any information from her previous purchases of years ago on the system. He had to call the computer department. Then, the inventory identification numbers wouldn't be accepted into the system. Once the technological problems were solved, she then had to find an elevator, go up three flights to the "customer service" desk, wait in line for 15 minutes to give the clerk her order and pay. Which then took another ten minutes to input. She said she spent more time trying to pay for the item than picking out her choices!

How simple is it for your customers to place orders? Are the order forms easy to read? Can she fill it out easily by herself? Do you have calculators available with tax charts? Do you make her wait in line for you to calculate the total, or can she figure the total then give you the order and payment? Do you accept credit cards? Do you offer 24-hour fax ordering? Is your fax number printed on your literature? To find out the ease of your ordering system, place an order yourself. And, ask your customers for requests.

Lemon Aid Links: Requests

MY OWN DEED IDEAS:

V

Vacations

This is not a section on having you take a vacation, although you do need to schedule some renewal time away from your business. No, as usual, I've done the *TWIST*.

Have you ever felt that summer time can be a slump time? Vacation time for customers can put a crimp in your business and profits if you don't plan ahead and promote *their going on-- vacation.* This idea works for both retail establishments and presentation plans. At the beginning of vacation time (or any holidays when you typically see a decline in business and attendance), do a **Post Card Contest promotion**. Notify your customers that you want to hear all about their vacation destinations. Instruct them to send you a post card from their vacation. Once a month, or at your choice of other intervals, do a drawing for free merchandise. You can also give recognition for the closest destination (not everybody goes far away, and this will encourage your customers to participate even if they are on a weekend get away), the farthest, the most exotic (one you've never heard of), the most unique (for the only customer who went to that particular place), or whatever other recognition you want to give.

How will this help build your business?
You will know when they have returned from vacation so you can call to discuss new business, set up demonstrations, or visit with them about your business opportunity. A simple phone call to thank them for sending the post card opens a lot of doors!

Now you know one more important fact about your customers that you can talk with them about. "Megan, how was Washington, D.C.? Thanks for the postcard. Did you visit the Smithsonian while you were there?" Simply another icebreaker.

Many people plan on pre-paying for their trip but sometimes succumb to plastic. You can now offer your company's opportunity to help pay the bills!

For customers who do not go on vacation, invite them to send you a postcard describing in words or pictures their "dream destination" if time or money were not a consideration (the two reasons we don't go on vacations!). Now you know their desire, could your product/service/opportunity help them realize their dream? Or, is your company offering an incentive trip to their desired destination?

To increase the number of postcards you receive, hand out pre-printed address labels and a postcard stamp. Promote this contest on all literature you give out, at all presentations, with flyers in your place of business, and on your answering machine/voice mail.

Voice Mail

Voice mail is really just an answering machine inside your phone. For businesses, I recommend this in place of a tangible machine for several reasons.

First, you can retrieve messages remotely from any phone. Many answering machines have this feature, but I've never had them work as well. Voice mail seems to have fewer glitches.

Second, you can get additional mail boxes to give your callers specific options. If they want information on your products, put this in one box. Information on your opportunity, another one. This way callers listen to what they want to hear, not what they have to hear.

The best part is you can avoid "call interrupting." This is my term for call waiting. I'm an advocate for call waiting in my home so that if my kids need to get in touch with me, I'll be notified. However, when I am on the phone with a client, I want all my attention focused on that conversation. On the other hand,

I don't want other customers calling me and getting a busy signal. So, those calls that come in are routed to my voice mail box. After every conversation, I check for new messages that might have come in. Some systems will actually tell you that you have new messages.

If you choose voice mail, or an answering machine, just have some way of receiving and retrieving messages. I am really surprised at the business owners whose phones I call with no type of message system. One lady used the excuse that she had caller ID in place of an answering machine. If potential customers call (as I called her), they don't know if they have reached you or not. You are missing out on free advertising opportunities as well as demonstrating that customers are important to you.

Lemon Aid Links: Answering Devices, Telephone Tips

MY OWN DEED IDEAS:

Waiting List

As you establish yourself as an expert and professional in your field, you will become a magnet for new customers. Your schedule will be full, and the demand for your expertise will increase. You will need to create a waiting list to be able to service and meet with everyone who wants you. This is actually going to be a tool to add new business.

If you can't fit someone in your schedule or they can't fit you in theirs (notice the *TWIST*?), put their name and phone number on a waiting list. When you have an opening, or need to fill in a slot, call these leads and tell them you just had a time slot open and you can fit them in. Even if they weren't waiting for your call, or don't need your service/product at that moment, they will agree to meet you because they know it might be their only chance. This is because you positioned yourself as a busy, sought-after person.

Lemon Aid Links: Lists, Overbooking

Wish Catalogs

The concept of a "wish list" is common in many companies. To set yourself apart and to add more impact, go a step further and promote a **wish catalog.** When a customer writes down names of desired items on a list, it doesn't mean as much as **seeing a picture** of the product. Use a bold marker and write (or have a stamp or sticker designed that says), "Wish Catalog." Your customer knows to keep this catalog in a safe place. Give her special stickers or a highlighter to mark all the items she wants. Remind her that money is no object in the wishing process.

MY OWN DEED IDEAS:

X

X-Ray

Look deeper than what you see; find out information about your leads. You don't need equipment that is radioactive, you just need to have alert eyes, ears, and heart to listen, observe, and feel for your customers. Then learn how you can help fill their needs and wants. When you know about your lead, you'll know how you can service him/her with your product/service/opportunity. Using this X-Ray technique, you'll see, hear, and feel wants and needs that are deeper than the surface. Find out by asking, not probing. Being Interested, not interesting.

MY OWN DEED IDEAS:

Y

You!

Earlier in the book, I said the most important tool in turning deeds into dollars is Follow Through. This is true. However, **none of these tools and ideas will work unless you do!** You are the master craftsperson, you are in charge, and in control. The success of converting leads to long-term customers and residual profits is in your hands.

MY OWN DEED IDEAS:

Z

Zest

Zest: Added flavor or interest, piquancy; charm. Spirited enjoyment, wholehearted interest, gusto. The outermost part of the rind of an orange or lemon, used as flavoring.

As you conclude this reading of The Lemon Aid Deed Book, I challenge you to add **zest** to your life and business. Become spirited about your business, present your products and opportunities with extra flavoring and wholehearted interest and gusto! Let this zest come through on the outside—like the lemon peel—so customers will feel your passion. And, as you do, you will enjoy many sweet successes and juicy profits!

When life (or business) gives you lemons, make something *better* from the bitter!

The Lemon Aid Lady
Christie Northrup

Add more
Sweet Successes And Juicy Profits
to your Business with these other
Lemon Aid Books

Did you begin your business by depending on your family and friends to be your customers? Has this pool of leads run dry? What do you do next?

Turn to the 113 pages of
The Lemon Aid Lead Alphabet:
Where to find Customers when you run out of Family and Friends
You'll learn how to:
- Build your business in *new neighborhoods*
- Use the world's *biggest and best lead book*
- Add profits to your bank account by reading the *newspapers and magazines*
- Advertise at *no cost*
- Do a *TWIST* on gathering–not just giving–*business cards*
- Create a *purse/pocket presentation*
- Locate leads in many more *unlikely places*

$19.95

Are your team meetings a **treat to plan?**
Is **attendance high** at your meetings?
Do your team members **look forward** to your meetings?
Does **performance increase** after a meeting is held?
YES will be the answers to all these questions when you plan meetings using the

TOTALLY TERRIFIC TEAM THEME BOOK
This book will give you
- 12 Fun Themes for planning Terrific Team meetings
- Six additional holiday/seasonal themes
- Invitation ideas for enticing members to attend
- Object lessons for reinforcing team training
- Challenges for follow through to increase performance
- Activities for involving each team member
- Reward Recognition incentives

$19.95

To order, call The Lemon Aid Lady, Christie Northrup, toll-free at
1-888-358-3001

Or send payment to: CANet Consulting, P.O. Box 1720, Lake Dallas, TX 75065. Add shipping/handling of $3.50 for one, .50 for *each* additional book; Texas residents add tax of 7.25%. VISA/MC/Discover accepted. Ask about corporate and quantity discounts as well as information on having The Lemon Aid Lady speak at your next event.

Prices subject to change without notice.

1-800-5-JENNY B

The Booster

WHAT IS THE BOOSTER?
ARE YOU IN A "PARTY PLAN"
OR "DIRECT SALES" BUSINESS?
DO YOU WANT TO
INCREASE YOUR
SALES & RECRUITS?
WE CAN HELP!
WE PROVIDE THE
"LITTLE THINGS" THAT MAKE
A BIG DIFFERENCE!

KEYS to SUCCESS

WE CAN HELP IN ALL THE
"KEY AREAS"
OF YOUR BUSINESS:
DATING/BOOKING, RECRUITING,
CUSTOMER SERVICE & MORE!

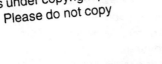

Visit our website:
http//www.
thebooster.com

CALL TODAY TO
JOIN
"THE BOOSTER CLUB"
& RECEIVE THE
"JENNY B" CATALOG
1800-553-6692

WE HAVE OVER 500 ITEMS TO
"BOOST YOUR SALES &
BRIGHTEN YOUR IMAGE!"
WE HAVE STICKERS, BUTTONS, POSTCARDS,
BOOKMARKS & MORE
TO BUILD & MOTIVATE YOUR TEAM!

CALL TOLL FREE 1-800-553-669